Becoming THE Expert

Enhancing Your Business Reputation
through Thought Leadership
Marketing

By John W. Hayes

HARRIMAN HOUSE LTD

3A Penns Road
Petersfield
Hampshire
GU32 2EW
GREAT BRITAIN

Tel: +44 (0)1730 233870
Email: enquiries@harriman-house.com
Website: www.harriman-house.com

First published in Great Britain in 2013

ISBN: 9781908003614

British Library Cataloguing in Publication Data
A CIP catalogue record for this book can be obtained from the British Library.

Set in Minion Pro and Gotham Narrow.

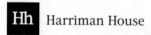 Harriman House

Printed and bound in Great Britain by
Marston Book Services Limited, Didcot

Contents

About the Author

John W. Hayes has been helping small and medium-sized companies develop their business strategies online for almost as long as the internet has been in the general public's consciousness. Working alongside some of the biggest names in ecommerce and online marketing (including Amazon, eBay and Google), he has dedicated much of his career to demystifying the web and highlighting growth opportunities for a diverse range of businesses. As the author of numerous white papers, blog posts and guest editorials across a wide range of trade and mainstream publications, he is widely recognised as an influential Thought Leader in the SME online marketing arena.

He divides his time between his office in London and his home in North East Lincolnshire where he lives with his partner Sarah and two daughters Rose and Dotty. When he is not at work or hanging out with the family, you can find him on his bike, cycling along a route by the sea and dreaming up his next big idea.

For updates on this book and future projects you follow him on Twitter: **@john_w_hayes** or on Facebook: **www.facebook.com/becomingtheexpert**

Preface

I started my career in the newspaper industry, working as an advertising sales representative for a small regional publisher owned by the British-based Northcliffe Media Group. It was while working for Northcliffe (around the mid-1990s) that I was first introduced to the internet. At the time, only one computer, in an office of approximately 100 fellow employees, had access to the web. The connection came via a 14K dial-up modem and you can believe me when I say that this did not provide the superfast broadband experience that we expect and enjoy today.

I had to ask permission to use the single internet-enabled PC, which was located (but never used) in the Sales Director's office, after being asked by a client to take a look at his website. The site turned out to be little more than a logo and a telephone number (not even an email address – so few people had them at the time) but still seemed to take forever to download. Little did I know that this request would soon take me away from the drudgery of advertising sales and start me down the path to a whole new career in an industry that, at the time, I didn't even know existed.

My curiosity about cyberspace (as we called it back then) led me to be singled out as the office geek and I was promptly promoted (without any consultation or wage increase) to the newly created position of New Media Manager (or Internet Champion, as it was referred to internally).

Armed only with a *HTML for Dummies* guidebook, I started planning, building and monetising online editorial and commercial platforms. The internet speed was slow, editors and journalists were reticent to have their articles published online, and advertisers laughed at the idea of spending money on a medium that virtually nobody had access to. It was a time of great uncertainty, but also one of great opportunity for those willing to take a chance; I loved every minute of it.

My work with Northcliffe took me to live in Budapest, where I continued to build newspaper websites for the company's portfolio of titles in central and eastern Europe. During this time I also began writing a weekly technology column for an English-language publication aimed at the expatriate business community who had flooded into the region after the fall of communism.

After five years I returned to live in England and continued to work for Northcliffe as a consultant. Alongside this work I helped a number of small and medium-sized businesses take their first steps online, lectured in online journalism and online marketing, traded on eBay, managed a series of affiliate marketing programmes, and began writing for a range of publications including the *Daily Mail*, *Yorkshire Post*, the *Sun*, *News of the World* and *Traveller*, easyJet's inflight magazine.

I had no formal training in any of these disciplines – it was just a case of reading up on a subject, making a few educated guesses and then giving it a go. You might say I studied at the Online University of Thought Leadership. In this respect I owe more to carefully crafted blogs and websites from the likes of Econsultancy (**www.econsultancy.com**) and EcommerceBytes (**www.ecommercebytes.com**), thriving community forums like A4uForum (**www.affiliates4u.com**), and the virtual bookshelves of **Amazon.com**, than any schooling. I'm not sure if it could happen today, but the early days of the internet were carved out by enthusiastic amateurs (of which I was very much one).

While helping a struggling catalogue company to reinvent themselves as an online retailer, I was introduced to ChannelAdvisor, a US-based technology company that had recently set-up shop in the UK. Although impressed with their software, it was the Thought Leadership presented by ChannelAdvisor's CEO Scot Wingo in his book *eBay Strategies* that sparked my interest in the company. Wingo's style of Thought Leadership, which extended through his blogging and speaking appearances, made what could have been a dry and data-heavy experience entertaining and informative.

I joined ChannelAdvisor in 2007 as their UK-based Product Marketing Manager and started producing a wide range of Thought Leadership content for the European and Australian markets. Encouraged to experiment with distribution channels, I produced white papers, blog posts, PR articles, podcasts, webinars, a pioneering series of videos for YouTube, and hit the road with the touring series of Insite events.

During this time, I formed strong relationships with some of the biggest names in ecommerce including eBay, Amazon and Google, who helped add credibility to my Thought Leadership campaigns and distribute them to a much wider audience.

While at ChannelAdvisor, I started using iContact, an email marketing application primarily targeted at small and medium-sized businesses. I had used several other email marketing tools in the past but never really felt like a valued customer of any of them until I discovered iContact. What made me feel so welcome? They picked up the phone and talked to me. I was dealing with humans and not just technology. In the online world this is not always so apparent.

I then joined iContact in the spring of 2011, where I used my experience to help evangelise about the company's technology and corporate ethos, helping to develop the brand for the European market.

Building on the strength of my relationships and in-depth knowledge, I have written for a wide range of industry publications and websites including *Internet Retailing*, *The Marketer*, *Direct Marketing News*, *Fourth Source*, *uTalkMarketing*, *Tamebay*, *Figaro Digital*, *Business2Community* and *Fresh Business Thinking*, as well as regularly producing content for the iContact Official Email Blog.

Who is this book for?

This book is for any entrepreneur, business owner or marketer who wishes to position themselves as a key influencer within their own particular field of expertise. It has been written to help you develop both basic and advanced Thought Leadership Marketing strategies. These strategies will help you raise your profile, build your reputation, generate leads and ultimately drive profits through the sharing of detailed knowledge and by engaging with the communities which you serve. It will be particularly useful to individuals and organisations that can prove themselves to be both agile and proactive.

We start this book by explaining what Thought Leadership Marketing is and who it is best suited to. We then move on to demonstrate how you can find and develop your voice before showcasing the various channels for distributing your Thought Leadership content.

A great many of the practices discussed in this guide are based on web-based technologies, but this doesn't mean it is only relevant to tech businesses or those who already have a well-developed web presence. The technologies examined here are accessible and in areas where there may be complexities, a full list of useful resources and tips has been provided.

Thought Leadership Marketing is inclusive and with a little thought, I believe, can prove to add value to any type of business. I have personally worked with a diverse range of companies, from fresh fish merchants on Grimsby Docks to global vendors of highly complex software solutions, and the majority of these companies have benefited from Thought Leadership Marketing. It's all about understanding your customers, knowing what makes their lives difficult and responding accordingly.

In the first of the aforementioned examples, the fresh fish merchant taught a journalist how to dispatch and cook a live lobster. Similarly, the vendor of highly complex software solutions demonstrated how complex systems could in fact make life easier for their business clients by using video testimonials featuring customers speaking in the plainest English (occasionally in fairly inaccessible regional accents).

I've yet to find a single business that could not benefit from Thought Leadership. However, if you believe you fall into this category, send me a message on Twitter (**@john_w_hayes**); I'll be happy to prove you wrong and send you a couple of Thought Leadership ideas.

Chapter 1

An Introduction to Thought Leadership Marketing

" A penny for your thoughts" is a well-known English idiom that grossly underestimates the value of your opinion. The fact is, your thoughts could be worth quite a lot more than that.

Thought Leadership is one of the most valuable marketing tools available to today's entrepreneur. Not only is it affordable to all (it is largely free), it is also available to anyone with an opinion – and who doesn't have one of them?

Long favoured by the IT community, who were early adopters of many of the technologies used to distribute Thought Leadership, it is equally appropriate for any industry where expertise is valued.

So what is Thought Leadership Marketing?

Thought Leaders position themselves as experts in a particular industry or discipline and share their insight with a wider community. Thought Leadership Marketing takes this insight and uses it to build brand, generate leads and ultimately drive sales. When you see a reputed expert on a subject quoted in a news article, or a video on YouTube instructing you how to do a task, or a blog post offering insight into the latest trends or advances in a particular industry, this is very often part of a wider Thought Leadership Marketing strategy. They are positioning themselves as experts and hopefully setting themselves up as a potential business partner for interested parties.

A good Thought Leadership programme will help you to maximise results from your marketing budget. It should also go some way to reducing your reliance on dated business techniques, such as cold calling, while helping your business to shorten its sales cycle. By carefully positioning content, you will not only attract attention to your business but also help qualify leads (i.e. sort the wheat from the chaff) and even solicit enquiries and orders. Some businesses are built on very little more than great Thought Leadership and a good transactional website – although most of us will still have to pick up the phone and speak to the occasional prospect or client from time to time.

In this respect, you can think of Thought Leadership Marketing as your hardest working employee. You could hire someone to sit on the phone and call between 30 and 40 prospects every day, perhaps generating one or two warmish leads to follow up on. Alternatively, you could spend half a day writing an 800-word article, publish it to a blog or trade publication, where it can potentially be read by many thousands of readers, and have the leads come directly to you. Thought Leadership Marketing empowers individuals within corporations to evangelise outside of the normal constraints of marketing. It is agile, adds personality to a brand and is perfectly suited to the socially enabled (networked) world in which we live.

Undoubtedly, social media will play a huge part of your Thought Leadership strategy, but be warned, it is neither the foundation nor structural makeup of your programme. Many people are socially connected; few are Thought Leaders.

Openness as a great asset

It is the openness of Thought Leadership Marketing that truly sets it apart from traditional marketing.

Great Thought Leaders do not play at business with their cards close to their chest. They are happy to share detailed insight across a wide expanse of knowledge, offering tips, tactics and strategies, which they will then back up with data from within their own organisations. They are also not afraid to express an educated opinion based on their previous experience.

It might seem a little reckless to be so open with your organisation's insight and intellectual property, and it is true that while much of what you share will go on to help form wider opinion, some will occasionally come back to haunt the originator. Nobody said that Thought Leadership Marketing was risk free. This might raise some red flags with more cautious marketers. You might be afraid that by sharing detailed inside knowledge you will not only open your company up to increased competition, but also empower your clients to go ahead and do the job themselves. Don't let this put you off. By and large, the rewards of Thought Leadership Marketing will nearly always outweigh the risks.

Let's think about the following scenario:

> Undoubtedly, your competitors will be able to glean professional knowledge from your insight. But by simply hanging on to your coat-tails they risk being perceived as second-rate imitators. Imitation is fine but it doesn't earn the premium rewards enjoyed by the originator. Rather than fearing your imitators, you should be more wary of your competitors who are putting themselves forward and delivering their own Thought Leadership programmes. How are they positioning themselves? How good is their insight? What kind of personality do they portray? What is their timing like? Do they trump you? If so, there is a real risk that you could look like the imitator; it's time to step up to the mark and strive to do a better job yourself.

As for customers taking your insight and doing the job themselves, picture this:

> You're a painter and decorator. You've written a blog post, which I've stumbled across, telling me how to hang wallpaper. You've told me what paper to buy, what paste to use, how to prepare my walls and all the professional tips I need to know to ensure the paper looks perfect when hung. You've even included videos demonstrating the more difficult aspects of the task and high resolution photographs of the finished job.

After reading this, do you think I'm going to hang my own wallpaper?

No way! I'm going to pick up the phone and ask you to do it for me. Why? Because you have shown me that you know what you are talking about and are not afraid to put your work under public scrutiny. In short, you are a Thought Leader and I trust you to get the job done right.

OK, this is perhaps a very simple example – but the complexity could be scaled to cover any industry. In the same way I might not be able to hang wallpaper, I might not have the time to file my own tax returns, have the resources to manage a portfolio of property investments, or the technical knowledge to install a new computer system.

It is the maverick nature of Thought Leadership Marketing that makes it so accessible to the target audience. By placing an individual at the forefront of an organisation, you can humanise even the most seemingly dreary industries and turn business leaders into household names.

While most of us will never see international fame, it is entirely possible to become a star in your own niche. Think about it, no matter what industry you are in, there will always be a familiar go-to person who the media (either bloggers, trade press, local or national media) always seem to turn to for a quote, piece of analysis or interview. These people are Thought Leaders and there is no reason why you cannot steal a bit of their thunder with some careful positioning.

Who are the Thought Leaders?

Thought Leadership is a diverse and multi-facetted discipline. It offers a number of strategies that can be adopted, regardless of the industry you work in. The best way to demonstrate this is to list ten prominent Thought Leaders who I believe have mastered the practice and who I regularly look to for inspiration (both inside and outside of business). Some of the names in this list will be instantly recognisable, others may be more difficult to place.

If you want to see how the pros do it, I suggest you seek these people out, learn how they use Thought Leadership to promote their business or celebrity status (remember celebrity is more often than not a front for business activity) and effectively position themselves at the top of their game.

- Jamie Oliver (celebrity chef and campaigner) – uses Thought Leadership via his regular TV appearances and magazine articles to promote the sale of his books and fill his ever expanding empire of restaurants.

- Micheal O'Leary (Ryanair CEO and raconteur) – never afraid of using a sound bite to fill seats on his budget airline.

- Steve Jobs (founder of Apple) – the man who made the computer and mobile telephone industry sexy.

- Marc Benioff (chairman and CEO of cloud computing company **Salesforce.com**) – the software man who hates software and wants us all to live in the cloud.

- Seth Godin (author and marketer) – probably the world's most inspirational and popular marketing guru.

- Martin Lewis (broadcaster and editor of Money Saving Expert) – started **www.moneysavingexpert.com** to help people save money and it made him millions.

- Simon Calder (travel writer and broadcaster) – the go-to person for people on the go.

- Marc Coker (founder of **Smashwords.com**) – behind the company that is shaking up the publishing industry one book at a time.

- Jeff Bezos (founder and CEO of Amazon) – the man who shaped the way we buy books, CDs, DVDs and virtually everything else online.

- Martha Swift and Lisa Thomas (founders of The Primrose Bakery) – the original UK cupcake entrepreneurs and bestselling authors.

Are you a Thought Leader?

To find out whether you have the potential to be a Thought Leader ask yourself the following questions. If you answer yes to them all, you are halfway to Thought Leadership.

- Do I possess a detailed knowledge of the industry I work in?

- Do I have an opinion about various topics within my industry?

- Do I have the ability to communicate my opinion effectively (either written or verbally, although preferably both)?

- Am I able to demonstrate my opinion is worth listening to, using case studies or references?

It is important you answer these questions honestly. Many people try and position themselves as Thought Leaders without the right credentials. Some even get away with it and make a name for themselves, often at the expense of people seeking quick wins and get rich quick schemes – the internet is full of these. Don't be tempted to do this yourself – your reputation cannot stand the risk.

Experience is the only thing that makes Thought Leadership credible. If you've got it, then you should go for it. If you haven't, put this book down for now and pick it up again in a couple of years when you have built up more experience.

Typical reservations about Thought Leadership

I speak to a lot of people who tell me they believe Thought Leadership Marketing would benefit their business significantly. They buy into the concept that it could not only help position their business as a significant player in their vertical, but also help to reduce (or at the very least maximise potential from) traditional marketing and sales budgets. But when push comes to shove they fail to engage, normally hanging on to one of the following four excuses:

1. **No time:** Time is in short supply and you just cannot find enough of it to invest in building a solid Thought Leadership programme. There is a good chance you identify with this and believe it to be a valid excuse. But before you make this assumption, take a look at your day and ask yourself what you are doing that adds value to your business and what you are doing simply out of habit. How often do you check sales figures or other business related statistics? Similarly, how much dead time do you spend staring out of train windows or drinking coffee in airport lounges? How often do you find yourself updating Twitter or LinkedIn with other people's Thought Leadership? Are you really busy all the time or are you victim of procrastination? It's a hard habit to break – I know I can be guilty of this at times. Could you find an extra 30 minutes a day to dedicate to Thought Leadership? If you are struggling to find the time, set your alarm clock half-an-hour earlier in the morning and check yourself when you consider hitting the snooze button.

2. **Fear:** Like many others, you may be worried that your opinion isn't valid or your customers and competitors will find holes in your arguments. All Thought Leaders have these moments of self-doubt from time to time. Don't let this unfounded fear put you off. Instead, you should concentrate on the one thing that validates your position – your experience. Remember, it is highly unlikely that anyone of any importance or influence will single you out for attack or question your opinion. The worst case

scenario is that you'll be ignored. In this case, it's time to look at your Thought Leadership strategy, re-evaluate what you think is important and reconsider what you believe your target audience is looking for.

3. **No ideas/lack of imagination:** This is quite frankly a lazy excuse. Think about it for a minute – where do other Thought Leaders in your industry look for inspiration? The answer is staring you right in the face. Their customers. You speak to these people every single day. You know what makes their lives difficult and how your business can help solve their problems. If you find yourself short of ideas, try speaking to the people who pay your wages.

4. **Lack of presentation skills:** Thought Leadership need not be a solo effort. Ideally it will focus on one or two individuals within your organisation but that doesn't mean you cannot enrol other people to help you out. Perhaps someone in your company has a flair for writing and can help you to polish your copy. Perhaps another individual is more comfortable in front of a camera or speaking to an audience. There is no reason why they cannot present your findings on your behalf (we'll cover this more in Chapter 5, where we discuss empowering your colleagues). If you are a one-man band it might be worth engaging with a freelancer to help you improve your position (there are also ideas on where to seek such help later in the book).

But sometimes it's not the lack of skill or talent that prevents an organisation from developing and delivering a great Thought Leadership programme. Sometimes it is easier to sit back and invent roadblocks than raise your head above the parapet and shout "I have an opinion!"

Let's have a look at a couple of examples I have encountered where businesses imposed roadblocks upon themselves.

Self-imposed roadblocks

Roadblock 1: Trust and too much attention to detail

Organisation 1 was completely sold on developing a Thought Leadership Marketing programme. They worked in an extremely tight niche which didn't justify mass marketing techniques, but still wanted to communicate best practices – as well as present upsell opportunities – to their target audience. They had the resources to deliver detailed Thought Leadership across multiple channels, held a strong belief in the validity of their argument (and their argument was good) and they certainly didn't lack imagination or presentation skills. But when it came to delivery they just couldn't get the stuff out.

Their problem was two-fold. Trust was a major issue, with all content requiring sign-off from a senior manager who was rarely available. Secondly, they questioned everything in minute detail, tweaking, re-developing and ultimately delaying (or scrapping) every project.

As they were delaying their Thought Leadership campaigns, their competitors were competently pushing out fairly reasonable content. While this Thought Leadership from competitors would never set the world on fire, it would certainly have a bigger impact on their potential clients than the wall of silence published from the overly reticent firm. And while they kept their lips tightly shut, fiercely loyal customers would sign long-term contracts with their competitors for services which could have been provided by the mute organisation – if only they had been more vocal in their approach.

Roadblock 2: Cynicism

Organisation 2 had access to a great product, could beat anybody on price and still maintain a decent margin and, perhaps most importantly, they possessed a complete understanding of the industry in which they worked. As a family business, their reputation had been formed over several generations and while the current business owners had modernised significantly (adopting internet technologies not normally associated with such a traditional business) they had retained much of the charm and character afforded to them by their long history.

This organisation had two streams of revenue. The first was from a client base who they had been serving for years (although this market was in decline). The second was via mail order customers who were attracted to the business due to its geographic location, which had a great reputation for delivering high quality products (a real opportunity for growth).

Due to the local interest connection, the local media (which included a range of newspapers, magazines, radio and TV) could have been particularly important to developing this organisation's brand. You should never underestimate the importance of the local media, particularly now that local stories can have a global audience thanks to the internet.

The local media were in fact very keen to showcase the products and services of this local business. They wanted to position them as local ambassadors and, as such, catapult their reputation to new heights. But every approach by local journalists and feature writers was rebuffed.

The reason for this was, in my mind, quite ridiculous. The owner didn't want his 'mates' (many of whom also worked in the same industry) reading about him in the local paper, claiming, "They would never let me hear the end of it if my photo was splashed all over the *Telegraph*." As a traditional industry, the adoption of modern technology was treated with a degree of cynicism and mistrust by many of his industry peers and for foolish reasons he feared their reaction to his high-tech endeavours more than the loss of significant steams of new business.

Instead of building his business on his reputation, the owner seemed happier to pay for advertising and promotion that failed to ride on the local connection and had little impact other than adding significantly to the costs of running the business. This meant he was just one of many businesses struggling alongside competitors who didn't deserve to be in the same class. I check in with the proprietor every now and again and business is so-so, but it seems they are losing significant trade to newer firms in the area who are building their reputations through their more aggressive approach to Thought Leadership.

***

These case studies are instructive because they show that you should avoid putting up barriers like these in your business. The moral of both these stories is don't waste your time inventing roadblocks – just get on with your Thought Leadership.

Chapter 2

Finding Your Voice

reat Thought Leadership can be built on simple ideas and often starts with a basic but engaging conversation point. However, coming up with an initial conversation point that resonates with your existing and potential clients can be difficult.

Often the best ideas are built around delivering solutions to your clients' most immediate needs. If you don't know what makes life difficult for your clients, it's time you asked them – they will probably give you a list.

If you can demonstrate successfully that you understand the challenges your clients face, and are able to showcase ideas that could potentially help them reduce costs, save time, maximise resources and ultimately drive profits, you are well on your way to developing an engaging Thought Leadership strategy.

Turning Ideas into Thought Leadership

Good Thought Leadership Marketing ideas are a rare and precious commodity, so make a note of any you have as soon as they occur to you. As great ideas rarely come when you have a piece of paper to hand, it might be an idea to use your mobile phone to record new ideas by sending yourself a quick email or text message.

Compile all your ideas in one space (a whiteboard is a good idea) so you can review, edit and prioritise them. Having these ideas in clear sight at all times will also help you come up with new or improved ideas as your daily work patterns stimulate your thought processes.

If you struggle to identify your best ideas, float them past a trusted colleague or client. Try to remember that the best Thought Leadership strategies will always act as a guide to solve a particular issue or problem your clients face.

At this early stage, try not to think too much about how your Thought Leadership will be distributed. It is far more important to identify an engaging idea that delivers a workable solution to a common business problem for your clients.

As long as the subject remains relevant and accessible to your target market, a piece of Thought Leadership content can be refined and repackaged a number of times. A single idea can germinate into a whole host of Thought Leadership products. For example, a blog post can be reworked into a more lengthy white paper or presentation. These in turn can be the subject of press releases and can lead to wider publicity within the media. You shouldn't be too concerned about repetition, although you will want to check that your content remains fresh. There will always be new clients who will appreciate your advice, no matter when it was first deployed.

Planning your thought leadership products

You should plan and create a range of Thought Leadership products that will be attractive to people with differing levels of knowledge and who have dealt with your organisation at different stages of the sales process, that is to say, your long-term customers – those who have bought from you once before – and those who have not heard of you until now. This is because some people will be hoping to engage with your services because they haven't got the skills or knowledge that you possess, others might be as skilled and as knowledgeable as you are, but have limited time or resources to execute your strategies. Remember that people like to digest knowledge in many different ways. For some the written word is king, others might appreciate a series of audio recordings and for the visually stimulated nothing will beat video.

Do not try and dumb things down, but whenever possible use plain English and maintain a pattern that is understandable and easy to follow. You won't win any friends or influence anyone with overly complex tech talk or jargon.

Thought Leadership is often consumed away from the working environment; I myself often read business books while on the train or even by the swimming pool on holiday. In such cases I want to be able to sit back and enjoy my reading and not be bamboozled by overly complex strategies. Some people listen to podcasts on their daily commute. They want an easy flow of information that won't distract them so much that they miss their train stop or drive into the back of someone else's car.

For a great example of how complex issues are explained in layman's terms, pick up a copy of the weekend edition of the *Financial Times*. The *FT*'s journalists have a great appreciation of the fact that their readership is neither stupid, nor has a complete understanding of every topic that they report on. As a result, their readers are usually universally better informed and rarely patronised.

Your Voice

It is one thing to have the ideas to build a Thought Leadership programme on, but finding a voice to distribute these ideas is altogether another thing.

By your *voice* I mean the style and tone of delivery of your Thought Leadership programme. This should be based on your target audience and your perception of how they would like to receive your insight.

If you find yourself wondering what your voice should be, I can recommend only one remedy. Immerse yourself in the Thought Leadership of others. Read as much as you can by other experts who work in the same field as you. Seek out their opinions in the press, subscribe to their email newsletters and blogs, watch their videos on YouTube, download their podcasts, and whenever possible attend the conferences and presentations where they speak. Be sure to ask questions and take notes on the content and also on the style of delivery.

Of course, some people have a natural flair for writing or public speaking. Don't let these people intimidate you. Their ease of delivery comes with practice and the confidence they have in their message. Learn from them and then ask yourself how you could do better.

Try and dedicate a little reading time focused on your particular industry into your working day as often as possible. Reading every day will not only ensure you keep abreast of the latest trends, but also help you to understand what your competition is up to. If you make regular reading a priority, it will ensure you are not put off by the sheer volume of reading material you may be presented with.

Make it easy for yourself to find relevant articles by subscribing to RSS (Really Simple Syndication) feeds from your favourite blogs and online publications. It is also a great idea to set up news alerts via Google News (**news.google.com**) using specific industry terms and competitors' names, etc. Both of these tactics will mean any relevant content is delivered directly to your email inbox, making it highly accessible, as well as providing you with a deep archive of relevant opinion.

It is also important to cast your eye outside of your industry. A greater understanding of what is going on in the wider world, particularly with the economy, will help you better position yourself with a more sympathetic and reasoned voice. As an old newspaperman, I'm telling you to read the newspapers and find out what is going on in the world. When you are well-read, ideas – and the voice you need to use to present them – will come to you much more easily, which will help build you as a character in the eyes of your audience.

Finding someone else's voice

A lot of prospective Thought Leaders fall into the trap of not finding their own voice, but instead borrowing or stealing other people's Thought Leadership. These people are easy to spot and they offer very little in the way of their own original Thought Leadership. I refer to them as *wannabe* Thought Leaders.

How to identify a wannabe

A wannabe thought leader will:

- Constantly re-appropriate and quote other people's content, research and testimonials in their own articles and presentations.

- Re-tweet (on Twitter) already highly visible content, believing they are somehow delivering breaking news and insight.

- Post regularly on internet forums and in the comments sections of blogs, where they rarely add any additional value and merely deliver a plug for themselves.

- Persistently use cliché and industry buzzwords to confuse the reader and make them think that their line of work is more complicated than it is.

If you are not adding value to the conversation, then you are not a Thought Leader. But there is one thing worse than the wannabe – and that is the content farmer.

Content farming

Content farming is a relatively new industry designed to help companies improve their rankings on internet search engines like Google by providing a steady stream of fresh content to their websites, delivered as news or Thought Leadership. A business wanting to design itself as a Thought Leader might employ the services of a content farmer to provide it with content for its website to give the impression it is publishing new material regularly.

Content farming is not generally a good idea. Farmed content rarely comes from an organic or nurtured environment. It is more likely to be written by unqualified banks of writers churning out reworked copy taken from, at best, a legitimate Thought Leader or, at worst, previously farmed content.

I have had some bad experiences with content farming myself and will share two of these here.

Bad experience with content farming: 1

While advising a small digital advertising agency on their communication strategy, I was presented with a contract a former member of staff had arranged for the provision of content from an apparently reputable news agency. The signed and completely watertight contract guaranteed to provide a quantity of short, snappy blog posts, which were to be written around a series of previously agreed topics.

There was no problem with the quantity. Three times a week, 500 words of grammatically correct text would land in the marketing manager's inbox. The problem was that while this text might have been useful in generating a few extra visits to the company's website through search engine optimisation (SEO), this *keyword journalism* would do little to drive any new business.

In fact these articles, had they been placed on the company's website, would have done more to drive business to their competitors than anything else. It was the complete opposite of Thought Leadership, involving a bank of writers who would take five minutes to research (i.e. Google) original, insightful articles and rewrite them with little thought to personality or where the text originally came from. Occasionally articles would arrive which were directly quoting competitors' Thought Leadership. As a result, the company paid the equivalent, over a two-year period, of an executive salary for content they just couldn't use.

Bad experience with content farming: 2

The email marketing industry (particularly in the UK) is a relatively tight community. As competitors, we all attend the same industry events, read the same publications and chase many of the same customers.

I like to think of myself as fairly active within the community and while I am happy to have my Thought Leadership scrutinised and criticised by my peers (certainly within competitive circles), I would never have believed it possible to have a direct competitor feature and effectively endorse my work on their site.

But it happens more often than you would think, with one competitor in particular quite keen on aiding my position in the email marketing industry. I won't name and shame the competitor but a quick search of Google will reveal all.

At first my ego was slightly bruised. Despite the public facing nature of my role, I clearly wasn't making enough noise to make that much of an impression on them. They clearly enjoyed what I was saying, but they obviously didn't have a clue either who I was or who I worked for if they were so keen on featuring me so prominently on their website. Then again, I was delighted that my opinion and analysis was considered more worthy for publication than their own Thought Leadership.

But of course, my appearance on their site had nothing to do with my own rank and position or indeed the perceived quality of the content. It was farmed content, pulled from Google on the back of a few keywords and rewritten by an individual with no depth of knowledge or particular interest in the email marketing industry. They found an article I had recently produced, changed it enough so as not to appear plagiaristic and published it directly to my competitor's blog. Within minutes of being posted, the writer would be on the lookout for his or her next piece, which could be about property investment, agriculture, or even ballroom dancing. Content farmers are generalists and it shows in the quality of their work.

The right way to nurture content

If you really cannot find the time or you don't have the talent to produce your own content, it is possible to contract content production out to a trusted third party. There are two ways you can do this:

1. **Employ someone to ghostwrite content on your behalf and publish it under your own name.** In this case it is imperative that you trust the writer. You'll want to hire someone who understands your business and also has knowledge of the way you operate. You'll want to suggest topics and provide quotes or soundbites to give your Thought Leadership an air of authority and authenticity. You'll definitely want to check everything before it is distributed. It is always a good idea to have your ghostwriter sign a non-disclosure agreement (NDA). This will prevent them from telling competitors and customers, should you fall out, where the content actually comes from and will help to protect your good name.

2. **Employ someone as your official brand ambassador.** They will have their own reputation to enhance, and will maintain and produce content under their own name. In short, they will be your Thought Leader. In this case you'll want to engage a person who is a well-known figure in your industry and who has a broad knowledge of your business. You might consider someone taking a career break (a young mother for example), or a retired professional who wants to keep their hand in. It might also be possible to find a professional blogger or journalist who is willing to exchange editorial freedom for a regular pay cheque.

Drawing on freelance talent to help produce your content

If employing additional headcount is not an option, freelancers can help you out with a number of projects, ranging from blog posts and presentations, all the way through to high-end video or book production.

There are a number of sources for finding freelance workers, including:

- **Elance (www.elance.com):** An online marketplace connecting freelance workers with potential employers. The range of services available on Elance is staggering and ranges quite literally from accountancy to zoology. The most eagerly sought out services tend to revolve around technical work, such as website design, or sales and marketing-related subjects, including content production and design. A lot of the work conducted via the site is performed in developing countries and can therefore be very cost effective, although quality can wildly vary.

- **PeoplePerHour (www.peopleperhour.com):** A similar website to Elance, where small businesses hire top freelance talent by the hour, allowing them to remain flexible and lean while getting the job done.

- **oDesk (www.odesk.com):** A remote staffing solution for long-term working relationships.

- **Skills Hive (www.skills-hive.com):** A relatively new variation on the freelance marketplace theme, allowing employers to manage virtual teams of freelancers. SkillsHive's close ties to universities in the UK ensures access to a wide selection of student and graduate workers keen to build a portfolio of work.

The majority of these freelance marketplaces operate in much the same way as traditional online marketplaces such as eBay. Vendors list their wares (or in this case, services) and invite potential employers to contact them with proposals. Alternatively, you might list a job that needs doing and the freelancers will bid on the project. Freelancers are then rated and paid in just the same way you would with a retailer. Payment is normally taken in advance and held in an escrow account until the job is delivered and approved by the employer.

When hiring a freelancer you'll want to set expectations up front. Brief them properly on your required topic, style, length, frequency, etc. It will always be in your best interest to maintain a great relationship with your freelancer, but you should consider how you will protect yourself if that relationship sours. Never give them the keys to your reputation (i.e. protect your passwords).

Thought Leadership is always better when it comes from the source. Think about this before you go down the freelance route and work out what you can do yourself first – why not try producing your own content and then hire a freelancer to add a little polish? Remember, even the work of highly respected journalists and world-renowned authors rarely reaches a public audience without first undergoing the editing process. There is nothing wrong with a little bit of spit and polish.

Chapter 3

Thought Leadership Channels

Once you have found your voice, you'll need to find a platform to broadcast from. Throughout this chapter we will look at the pros and cons of developing a Thought Leadership programme over a number of channels and examine how these channels interplay with each other. Some channels will offer greater credibility than others (which we will discuss later in this chapter), but none will harm your business as long as the arguments presented are solid (i.e. can be backed up with evidence and testimony) and the delivery is executed in a professional manner.

Modern technology, particularly the internet, provides numerous opportunities for your Thought Leadership to be heard. While your efforts shouldn't be entirely focused online, it provides an excellent starting point.

Thankfully, many internet tools allow even the most technophobic to present their insight in a professional manner. If you do find technology too daunting, you can always refer to one of the online freelance marketplaces, referenced in the previous chapter, from where you will be able to hire experienced people to help you.

Top tip

All of the channels mentioned in this book are just methods of delivering content. While you can improve the aesthetics of your Thought Leadership using professional design or production skills, this will not improve the quality of message. Sloppy Thought Leadership will penetrate any veneer, so it is important to get the message right before you start playing around with bells and whistles.

Blogging

The first Thought Leadership channel we will look at is blogging. Everyone's method for generating Thought Leadership content varies, but getting an initial concept down on paper first, to be developed later, should be your number one priority. Blogging is an ideal way to begin this process.

I personally like to start with an idea or concept that can quickly be turned into a blog post. While a blog post can be any length, I aim to produce short, snappy posts of anything between 300 and 800 words, which can be easily read on a computer screen. Ideas generated from a quick blog post can then be re-worked into a longer and more detailed white paper, which the reader will probably want to print out to read.

The white paper may then lead to a presentation or be summarised into a Press Release (driving downloads of the white paper). Presentations can then easily be turned into videos or podcasts. Very occasionally a simple blog post will grow into a full length book. Indeed, my motivation for writing this book stems from a number of conversations I had around a short post I wrote for iContact's blog entitled 'Believe in Yourself – You Are a Thought Leader'.

A blog post can act as a proof point for your Thought Leadership concept. Does your idea flow? Can it be easily digested by the reader? Will it spark debate? Will people want to share it? If the answer is "No" then it is likely you will have wasted very little time or resource in producing it. In this case, throw it in the bin and take another look at your whiteboard for another idea. If the answer is "Yes" then you can quickly publish it, analyse the feedback and then, if you believe the idea has wings, develop the message further.

Why would a business have a blog?

Every business worth its salt should have a blog. The reason for this is that the benefits of running a well-maintained and regularly-updated blog are extremely numerous. Let's look at some of the more important facts:

1. **Blogging gives your business a pulse:** The internet is littered with millions of static websites that do little to reassure the visitor that the business behind them is in good health. By blogging you not only demonstrate that your business is alive and kicking, but also that it is up to speed with the latest trends and best practices. This puts you in prime position, if your content is worthy, to serve customers' needs.

2. **Google loves a blog:** Internet search engines pick up on regularly updated content and this effect is multiplied when other trusted websites create links back to it. A good blog should be the cornerstone of your SEO (search engine optimisation) strategy, driving free traffic to your website.

3. **It is social media fuel:** Your blog posts will provide valuable content for your own and other people's social media output. People just can't resist sharing incisive blog content – it makes them feel, in their own small way, like a Thought Leader.

4. **It places you at the centre of your community:** A good blog post will generate feedback from readers, which will boost your SEO rankings (see point 2) and help to build a community around your Thought Leadership, bringing people back to your site again and again.

5. **Blogging can place you first past the post:** The ease and speed of blogging means you can react quickly to situations, giving you a first-move advantage and tying your comment to an emerging piece of news or an important trend.

What makes a good blog?

Perhaps it would be easier to explain what makes a bad blog, because there are plenty of them out there.

But let's stick with the positive. A good blog is regularly updated with content that is both relevant and interesting to your client base. Some people make the mistake of believing they have to humanise their blog by writing articles about their life outside of work. While it is perfectly acceptable to drop in the occasional post highlighting an employee's personal achievement, or activities outside of the company's normal mode of operation – such as a charity event you have supported – nobody wants to read about your recent holiday to Majorca or early morning adventures with public transport. It's best to just get straight to the point and not risk distracting your readers with unfocused content – it will confuse them and very likely drive them away from your business.

Five great ideas for blog posts

1. **Top tips:** Everyone loves reading top tips around a topical issue. The number of tips you provide is irrelevant; don't try and force ten mediocre tips when three great ones will do.

2. **Case studies:** Use your blog to highlight a customer success story.

3. **News:** Product launches, customer wins, new hires, partnership announcements and awards all make great news stories.

4. **Opinion:** Everyone has got one, so put the world to rights and let people know where your business stands on your blog.

5. **Images:** Share images and photos from your latest projects via your blog.

A crash course in blogging

Along with many other aspects of Thought Leadership, when it comes to blogging nothing beats a little trial and error. If you've got an opinion, or if you've got something you want to share, you might as well get some skin in the game and start blogging. The eight simple points below should help you on your way.

1. **What's the point of what you are saying?** A good blog post should always have a purpose. This could be sharing a piece of news, an opinion, a concept or an idea around a subject. Before writing and ultimately publishing, you should ask yourself the following: Will my readers gain any value from reading this? A great way of answering this question is to ask: Would I like to read this myself?

2. **Link to the good stuff:** A blog post should be easily digestible, but capable of imparting wider knowledge should the reader wish to explore further. You can do this by linking to complementary blog posts or web pages. Be careful when linking to third-party blogs or websites that you are not pushing your readers away to a competitive Thought Leader – it might be hard to win them back. It's good practice to have third-party links open up in a separate browser window, so that your blog isn't lost when the reader navigates away from your content. Most blogging platforms will allow you to easily select how you want to deal with your links.

3. **Get to the point:** Don't waste your readers' time with waffling prose. A good guideline is to keep your blog posts to between three and five paragraphs in length, for example:

   - **Paragraph 1**: Introduction

   - **Paragraph 2-4**: Problem/solution

   - **Paragraph 5**: Key takeaways/conclusion

4. **Images:** Always try to use good images to run alongside your blog post. Whenever possible these should be your own images (never use one pulled at random from the internet). If you do need a source of photos because you have not got your own,

Flickr (**www.flickr.com**) is a good source of free images that can be used under the Creative Commons license. (**www.flickr.com/creativecommons**). iStockphoto (**www.istockphoto.com**) and Stock.XCHNG (**www.sxc.hu**) also provide excellent resources for low-cost and free images.

If you have access to a designer it might be an idea to illustrate a blog post with an infographic. An infographic is a visual representation of information, data or knowledge, which can be digested quickly and easily.

5. **Moving pictures:** Video is an excellent complement to your written content. It can also help improve your chances of being discovered on the search engines. We will cover video in greater depth later in this chapter.

6. **Keywords, phrases and headlines:** Before writing you'll want to give some thought to the various keywords and phrases you should use throughout your blog post to improve its chances of being found by search engines. Try and imagine the various keywords potential customers will use when they are searching the internet for help and advice on a particular topic. The real challenge is to then work these terms into readable content.

Good content writers understand how to write for both a human and the computer-based systems that control the search engines. Gaming the system in such a way is part of that larger topic of search engine optimisation (SEO), which we have referenced a couple of times already. Mastering even the basics of SEO is a book in itself. However, Google provides an excellent document for beginners (**bit.ly/GoogleSEOguide**). Blog headlines should not only feature prominent keywords or phrases but also tell the complete story in one short sentence. A good headline can be your one and only chance to grab a reader's attention, so it needs to be catchy and intriguing.

7. **Call to action:** Remember your blog has a greater purpose than just to tell a story – it is there to drive business. Every page should therefore have a call to action. This could be a reminder to pick up the telephone and call you, a form to send an email, a newsletter subscription form, the invitation to connect via social media by asking them a question, or even a buy it now button; or preferably all five. Getting them to question how your Thought Leadership can improve their business will improve the chances of them picking up the phone or dropping you an email to ask for your help. Too many people fail to integrate their corporate blog into their business properly and, as a result, waste countless opportunities to convert Thought Leadership into paying business.

8. **Encourage debate:** Don't be afraid to use the comments section of your blog to encourage debate around your Thought Leadership. Comments will help with your SEO as they add additional content to your blog. They will act as inspiration for future blog posts and may even generate sales leads as people post comments looking for your help and advice. Most blogging platforms allow you to vet comments before they appear on your blog. If you are worried about competitors or internet trolls hijacking your comments, you should enable these controls, remembering to check regularly for new comment to ensure a decent flow of content.

Example Blog Post

The following blog post demonstrates a number of blogging best practices. I have tried to keep it entertaining and informative. Experience has taught me the phrase "social media marketing" in the headline is a great driver of traffic and the mention of a celebrity name will also aid visibility via both the major search engines and social networks.

The boilerplate at the bottom of the article serves several purposes; helping to better position myself as a Thought Leader, promote the company I work for (linking the company name will also aid SEO) and increase awareness of the book you are currently reading.

Dynamic, Simple and Clean Email and Social Media Marketing – Courtesy of Gordon Ramsay

I'm told I'm pretty lucky when it comes to content creation. Ideas come to me fairly easily. They are not always great ideas – but they come along in rapid enough succession to enable me to separate the wheat from the chaff and produce a fairly reasonable rate of useable content.

Conversely, many of my clients at iContact tell me that they struggle to come up with creative ideas to keep their email and social media campaigns engaging. They tell me that content creation is time consuming and, when ideas don't come easily, can often appear a little forced.

Like I say, I'm lucky. But I believe I create my own luck.

So where do my ideas come from?

The answer is pretty much anywhere and everywhere. They come from customers, colleagues, competitors and other industry peers. Sometimes they come from completely out of the leftfield. The secret is knowing how to capture these ideas and record them before they disappear (ideas can be precious and fleeting so never ignore them when they come along).

For example, the idea for this short blog post came while watching a late night repeat of Gordon Ramsay's television show *Kitchen Nightmares USA*. In between Chef Ramsay's potty-mouthed outbursts and close ups of inedible food came three words describing what type of cuisine the desperately failing restaurateur should be aiming for: *Dynamic, Simple and Clean*.

My initial thought was, *Dynamic, Simple and Clean*, wow he could be speaking about Email Marketing! I picked up my mobile phone and quickly sent myself an email with the subject line: *Dynamic, Simple, and Clean*. I then turned the television off, retired to bed and forgot all about email marketing (I love my job but I'm not so sad that I dream about it).

Had I not emailed myself Chef Ramsay's words of wisdom, I wouldn't be sitting here writing this blog post and perhaps I'd be struggling to come up with something else.

Remember content, like the ingredients of a fine meal, is best when it comes from an organic and nurtured source (never forced farmed). You can help develop your email and social media marketing strategies by recording nuggets of everyday conversations with colleagues and customers, as well as outside influences such as blog posts, newspaper articles and television programs.

No good idea ever came from staring at a blank screen. So widen your sphere of influence, look at things with an open mind, and when inspiration comes – write it down (or send yourself an email as I did). With a bank of good ideas, you'll find developing a creative email and social media marketing strategy comes so much easier.

Author

John W. Hayes is the EMEA Business Development Executive for iContact (part of Vocus), the Email Marketing and Social Media Marketing for Small and Medium-sized businesses. He is also the author of Becoming THE Expert: Enhancing Your Business Reputation through Thought Leadership Marketing *which is available for sale at Brightword Publishing.*

This blog post was originally published on Business 2 Community:

www.business2community.com/online-marketing/dynamic-simple-and-clean-email-and-social-media-marketing-courtesy-of-gordon-ramsay-0182841

Blogging summary

The power of blogging should never be underestimated. I have had the pleasure of working with several bloggers who have turned homemade blogs into significant, cash generating businesses. If this sounds interesting to you, watch this space (or follow me on Twitter).

One of the main benefits of blogging is the fact your content doesn't have to conform to the editorial scrutiny and agenda of a commercial news site. The opinion embedded on your blog is clearly your own and is as credible as your argument makes it. However, a little third-party scrutiny will certainly add to your credibility. Therefore, it is hugely beneficial to provide guest editorials to more widely read trade publications and sites, in addition to publishing on your own blog. Consequently, guest editorials are the second channel we will look at.

Guest editorials

Publishing a guest editorial in a respected trade journal or on a third-party blog can add instant credibility and reach to your Thought Leadership programme. Building relationships with bloggers and journalists should also be seen as the vitally important first steps in a wider public relations strategy (which we will discuss in the next section of this chapter). You should target publications and blogs that are of interest to you and your potential client base. If you are unsure how to select these target publications, ask a small group of customers which publications they regularly read and which journalists/bloggers they respect.

Writing your first guest editorial

As you write your first guest editorial you have to bear a number of issues in mind:

- **Is this article relevant to the readership?** How advanced is the readership of the site or publication you are hoping to submit to? There is little point in offering a beginner's guide to an advanced group of industry experts. Similarly, if you over-pitch to a readership of enthusiastic amateurs you will probably disengage them.

- **Am I adding value to the conversation?** It doesn't matter what angle you take as long as you are adding value to the debate around a particular topic. If you are turning over old ground or reaffirming someone else's Thought Leadership, it's time to rethink your article.

- **Get to the point:** Does the editorial have a clear and actionable point? Don't waste the readers' (or journalists') time with articles that go nowhere. Always make sure you challenge the reader to take action (even if that is just to reconsider their current behaviour).

- **Does this sound like an advertisement?** Advertising copy does not make good Thought Leadership.

The fact is, websites, magazines and journals will not feature editorial that doesn't conform, within their guidelines, to the above points. Journalists, editors and bloggers are all busy people, and they love it when someone they know and trust can provide them with good clean copy that they can publish after a cursory glance. If you send them something they have to work on, the chances are they'll never read another submission from you again, so make your submission a good one and you may be asked for more material in the future.

You should also research the following about your target publication:

- **The nature of the publication:** Take note of readership, style and average article length.

- **Journalist/blogger names:** Get to know them. Seek them out at industry events.

- **Deadlines:** This is particularly relevant to print publications which are often planned many months in advance. There is no point in delivering a Christmas story in November when the magazine is working on its March edition.

- **Other guest writers:** Who else do they publish? Could you add to the argument of another Thought Leader or perhaps fill a hole in a particular niche with your area of expertise?

- **Do they accept advertisements?** You can often fast track the affections of a publisher or journalist with a little advertising budget.

Making the approach

When you first approach a publication, it is not always a good idea to pitch your ideas straightaway. Tell them you enjoy their work, comment on a particular article and suggest you might have something of interest to them further down the line. Good writers live and die by their carefully formed relationships, but they can be very suspicious of out and out PR pitches – so it is always best to try approaching them with a little finesse.

Never forward a completed article for publication without first asking permission to do so. Sending in an unsolicited article is tantamount to spamming the journalist, who will probably not get past your opening paragraph (if they even open your email). You should always ask first if they accept guest posts and then make a suggestion regarding the topic. Also, ask the journalist to give you the required word count, deadline and any other information that you will find useful when supplying the article, and then write your piece accordingly.

Try and conform to any requests the publication makes. If they ask for 800 words, try and hit a number within a 50 word threshold on either side of this number (closer if it is for a print publication where physical space is an issue). Most importantly, you should stick rigidly to any given deadline. Nothing will cause more damage to a nascent relationship with a journalist than late copy.

It is best practice to supply the text of your article within the body of an email (i.e. not as an attachment). This prevents any issues with formatting which might be caused by running different word processing programs and also ensures the article can be read on any device as soon as it is submitted. Send your text along with a good-quality photo of yourself, any other relevant images or graphics and the details you would like to run alongside your by-line – such as your company name, job title, contact details, website address, etc. It is important to get this company information published with the piece if at all possible, otherwise it slightly defeats the object of the exercise.

Public relations (PR)

Developing a strong public relations strategy adds value to your Thought Leadership programme. Good PR should be proactive, helping you to create buzz around your industry, and reactive, helping your brand ride on the coat-tails of a news item or significant event.

PR can also help with damage limitation when things don't go so well. It's far better to be seen to be in control of a situation than let rumour fan the flames of controversy.

A good PR agency may wish to charge you a lot of money to handle your account, but it is perfectly possible to cost effectively manage your PR in-house. In fact, if you work in a niche industry where detailed knowledge comes at a premium, you will probably be more successful if you handle your PR yourself. This is also the case because good PR is built on relationships and it is highly likely that you will maintain these relationships yourself. Running your own PR will also allow you to turn items around quickly without going through a middle man, which would delay the process.

However, if your time is limited you may have to hire the services of a PR agency to handle these relationships for you.

On PR agencies

I've worked with a number of PR agencies over the years. Some have been good; some have been less than impressive.

A good PR agency should develop an understanding of your business, your products and your plans for the future. They should provide you with ideas for features and news articles, and come running to you when an opportunity in the media presents itself. They can only do this by spending time with you, talking to your customers and getting under the skin of your business.

When you work in a niche industry it can be particularly hard for even the most proficient agency to deliver creative PR around your brand or product without considerable input from the client. In such cases, you should consider whether your investment in time is matched or bettered by their extensive list of contacts.

Small businesses in particular should be wary of employing the services of a large agency, where they might find themselves de-prioritised by more prestigious clients on the agency roster. When this happens the agency will often farm your account out to junior members of staff, who may struggle on your behalf with limited resources.

PR, like many other forms of marketing, should be seen as a long-term investment. But this does not mean you should commit to a long-term relationship with a particular agency on the back of a few glowing references and a shiny corporate office. Set your expectations before signing any contract and make sure you are able to dissolve the relationship quickly and painlessly, should these expectations not be met.

In my experience, a small or boutique agency will be able to offer more sympathetic terms than a larger corporation (and will often match or even better the service as they are able to focus more resource for less money on your brand).

A small fish in a large pond

I once had the pleasure of working for an organisation that had the ambition to hire the services of an extremely large and prestigious London-based agency. Their fees matched their impressive client list, which included many household names and their highly desirable postcode. As we offered a niche product to a small but lucrative audience, our desire to be included on this agency's roster alongside these global brands was a little over ambitious.

At the beginning of the month I would be sent an email with a list of upcoming feature ideas and pitches the agency were working on. Halfway through the month I would be sent an update of how these pitches were progressing. Finally towards the end of the month there would be a 15-minute telephone call scheduled to discuss these activities. Needless to say, the call would normally start with an apology for the lack of success over the previous weeks. Once every three months I would be treated to an espresso coffee and a biscuit at their West End office suite. For this level of service the company paid the princely sum of £3,500 per month.

I wanted to sack the agency after six months due to this lack of activity, but the contract (which a predecessor had signed), tied us into an 18-month relationship.

Around £63,000 + VAT bought the company an interview on a local London radio station talking to a demographic who would never become a client, and a splash in a trade magazine featuring one of our clients in which our name was either never mentioned or cut by the magazine's editor. This was not a good investment and this should provide a warning to you if you are thinking of hiring a PR firm. Many businesses could spend this money more effectively, or achieve better PR with less of an outlay.

Press releases

The press release is perhaps the most obvious piece of kit in the PR toolbox. While it is not the be-all and end-all of PR, a well-constructed press release has many uses. A good press release can help you launch a new product or service, share news of a recent customer acquisition or the recruitment of a senior member of staff. It can also be used to announce the publication or release of an exciting piece of Thought Leadership.

Your press release can be distributed widely in shotgun fashion or targeted with laser focus towards a specific section of the media.

There are a number of online press release distribution companies, such as PR Newswire (**www.prnewswire.com**) and PRWeb (**www.prweb.com**), which will host your release online, deliver it to a targeted group of journalists, and guarantee your release is picked up by the major search engines, as well as a selection of online news sites. These sites are perhaps more effective as search engine optimisation tools than serious news aggregators. However, a well-written release with a catchy angle can be picked up by both the mainstream and trade press.

As with any form of Thought Leadership Marketing you should consider whether the content included in your press release is relevant, interesting and newsworthy before you release it. There are plenty of topics that fall into this group.

Six newsworthy ideas for your press releases

1. **New hires and company expansion:** Have you just recruited a new key member of staff to your organisation? Where did they work prior to joining your company? What have they achieved in the past? What major projects will they be working on for your company? It isn't just senior members of your team who can be newsworthy. If you are going through a period of growth and looking to expand your team with a series of hires, this is also extremely newsworthy, especially in an economic

environment where many businesses are struggling. As well as showcasing your business as strong and healthy, you will also attract resumes from potential employees, helping you to avoid some of the high costs associated with recruitment.

2. **Awards:** Have you, a member of your team, a product or service, just won a significant award? This is big news and definitely worth shouting about in a press release. If the award is prestigious enough, being short-listed might be newsworthy enough to warrant a release. If your peers think enough of you to put you up on a pedestal, don't be shy. Acknowledge your pride in being selected and thank your customers and employees for their support.

3. **Product launches:** Do you have a new product that solves a significant problem for your clients? Then you've got a news story. Try and back up the announcement with a good customer quote (perhaps referencing the results from a beta test) to add credibility to your release.

4. **Significant milestones:** Anniversaries, customer wins, acquisitions, rounds of funding, revenue growth, reaching profitability, etc., all make great news stories.

5. **Charitable contributions/environmental awareness:** Show the world you care about a little more than just the world of business and profits. Be careful here; your support of a charitable cause or environmental campaign must come from the right place. Any cynical exploitation of a good cause will not do your business any favours. Focus on the individual achievements of your staff or people you support, showcase the issues at hand and demonstrate your primary concern is improving the lives of the people and the environments in the areas where you, your customers, your suppliers and your employees live and work.

6. **Survey results:** A survey can provide an excellent base to build a press release around. Delivering insight collected from customers or another targeted group suggests you have a deep knowledge of a particular industry. Online services such as SurveyMonkey (**www.surveymonkey.com**) provide easy-to-use

tools for surveying groups of people and quickly collating the results. It is even possible to set up simple polls on social media sites, such as Facebook or LinkedIn, which will widen the coverage of the survey beyond your own database.

How to structure a press release

Press releases normally follow a standard format. A quick web search will reveal a number of templates you can use. Online services, like the aforementioned PRWeb, also provide templates to help you produce the perfect press release. While you shouldn't deviate from the standard template this does not mean your approach to carefully crafting a press release cannot be a creative one.

A press release should feature the following details:

1. **Your company logo:** If your company is well known this will make your release stand out.

2. **Identifier:** Identifies the document as a **PRESS RELEASE** – use clear, bold lettering.

3. **Release information:** This identifies when the content is available for release and normally states: "For immediate release". There is very little point in setting an embargo on a press release – would you trust a journalist to sit on an exciting piece of news knowing that it has already been sent to rival publications looking for a scoop? Also, if they want to use it they want to use it immediately, they don't want to put it to the side for later (they may forget it or something better may come in).

4. **Contact details:** This should include a name, job title, phone number and email address.

5. **Headline:** Short and attention grabbing, your headline should scream "Read me!"

6. **Sub-headline:** Expands on the headline. A good sub-headline will tell the entire story in a single sentence.

7. **Place line:** Identifies where the story is coming from. This is especially important if you are hoping to pitch the story as having a local relevance.

8. **Date line:** The date the press release was issued.

9. **Lead paragraph:** The lead paragraph should tell the reader the who, what, why, when and where of the story. It should include the name of the business, a website address and a brief explanation of what the business does. The place line, date line and lead paragraph should be rolled out together as follows: "**12/09/12 – London – Brightword Publishing, the UK's leading publisher of …**"

10. **Body copy:** Normally three to five paragraphs of copy that follow the lead paragraph and complete the full story. As the story progresses you should include a couple of quotes from someone within the company and, when possible, a client or industry expert. The final paragraph should be wrapped up with full contact details.

11. **Boilerplate:** A potted history about your company and services.

12. **End mark:** Your press release should end with a standard ### or –end–.

13. **More information:** Additional content that may be useful to journalists when writing a story based on your press release.

The right time at the right place

There is no guarantee a press release will earn you significant media coverage. Journalists receive numerous releases every day and yours will need to stand out if it is to make an impact. Building solid relationships with journalists, their editors and the publishers will improve the chances of your press release being picked up. However, there is another way you can stack the cards in your favour. There are certain times of the year, often referred to as *silly season*, when news can be in short supply and journalists may be keener to run items that normally wouldn't make the page.

Silly season peaks during the summer months and again between Christmas and New Year. In the past, I have personally used silly season to create opportunities to place rather unlikely stories in the press.

The elevator pitch

When dealing with journalists (or anyone else you meet in business), it is important that you maintain a consistent brand message describing what it is your company actually does. The constant repetition of this on-brand message will quickly cement your position as a provider of a particular service. There is little point in telling one journalist you are a house builder and then telling another you are a property developer. It will confuse people and make it difficult for your company name to resonate as a leader within a particular area. If you are somewhat of a jack-of-all-trades, then you should focus on the one or two lines of work that bring in the most income and build your brand message around them.

To help with this aim of having a snappy and consistent brand summary, you should create what is called an *elevator pitch*. This is a concise message explaining the nature of your business. It's called an elevator pitch because it is how you would describe your company if you had to introduce it to a stranger while taking a short ride in an elevator when you've got less than 30 seconds to impress them.

Once you have nailed down your on-brand elevator pitch, pin it somewhere within plain sight in your offices and don't forget to share it with your colleagues. You should reach for your elevator pitch whenever you are asked about what your company does; whether this is by a potential client, a journalist, or even a stranger in an elevator. The consistency will serve you well.

Become a source

Press releases are fine for pushing out your own news agenda, but to be truly useful to a journalist you need to become a trusted source. This, again, is all about building relationships with key journalists covering your particular industry, as well as the wider media.

There are a number of online tools that can help you become a useful source. If you are based in the UK you should look at the excellent ResponseSource (**www.responsesource.com**). Companies targeting US-based journalists can find a similar service in HARO – Help a Reporter Out (**www.helpareporter.com**). Services like ResponseSource and HARO are a PR firm's secret weapon. When a journalist needs a quote or an opinion, or an editor needs a complete by-lined article from an industry expert, they can post a request on ResponseSource or HARO, which is then emailed to a list of subscribers.

ResponseSource offers paid subscriptions covering media requests across a number of verticals. I have personally been a subscriber for a number of years and cannot recommend this service highly enough. There is rarely a week goes by where I haven't won media that pays for the entire annual subscription. HARO offers a free (freemium) product and a subscription model.

The opportunities that present themselves via these online services are varied and can range from requests to place your products in goodie bags given out at events, shout outs for magazine competition prizes, appeals for comment, or complete articles for print and online media, all the way through to requests to feature individuals and companies on TV and radio.

The relatively low cost of services like ResponseSource and HARO should mean that, with a little focus, the value of the PR generated easily covers the cost of your subscription.

White papers

For many technology companies, the white paper is the ultimate method of distributing Thought Leadership. But there is no particular reason why the white paper should be the sole preserve of the IT crowd. Remember, I believe that all of the methods of Thought Leadership discussed in this book can be adopted and exploited by a diverse range of businesses.

What is a white paper?

A white paper is a detailed document which is normally distributed online as a PDF. PDFs are used because they are quick and easy to create, maintain the same appearance no matter what type of machine they are viewed on and, perhaps most importantly, can be viewed independently of the software used to create them. Everyday software tools, such as Microsoft Word, are perfectly capable of creating PDF files. However, to produce a more readable document you should consider employing the services of a graphic designer to give the document a professional finish.

A great white paper should act as a guide or solve a particular problem and have the ultimate aim of helping the reader make a decision. While that decision will hopefully result in a sale, you should be careful not to be overly salesy. Thought Leadership is all about positioning yourself as an expert, not a salesperson. Instead, be sure to make it as easy as possible for the reader to follow up with you. Great Thought Leadership will improve your chances of this happening, but having a telephone number and an email address at the bottom of every page will obviously help too.

While a white paper should be detailed, try not to get too lost in the detail. Break your text up with graphics and bullet points to make it as easy as possible to read. Where possible, try to include customer testimonials and proof points. Always use plain English and explain any jargon. If you truly understand a subject you will be able to explain it easily without risk of losing the reader, who is relying on your Thought Leadership because they don't possess the depth of knowledge you have in your particular industry. If you try and blind people with science, you stand a pretty good chance of driving them away.

A photograph of you (or the author) will humanise your white paper and make you appear more approachable. You cannot underestimate the value of this. People buy from people they like and placing your face alongside your copy is a great way to introduce yourself as a new friend.

How a white paper is useful for you

Longer and more detailed than a blog post, the investment in time and money you put into the creation of a white paper means you shouldn't give it away without getting something in return. The standard payback of a white paper is the acquisition of some useful contact details, such as an email address or a telephone number, and other information that can be used as an actionable lead or starting point for future marketing campaigns.

Email marketing companies like iContact (**www.icontact.com**) provide all the tools you need to collect customer data and then direct newly-acquired contacts towards your white paper. You can do this by simply redirecting them towards a web page with a link to your PDF once they have entered their details. However, if you want to guarantee the quality of your data, you might want to set up a tool called an auto-responder (also available via services like iContact), which automatically sends an email with a direct link to your white paper once an interested party has registered their details.

Remember, not everyone who registers their details on your website and downloads your white paper will be a prospective customer. For example, a student might download the document for the purpose of research. But while they are probably not yet in the market for your product or service, they may act as an influencer as they discuss your Thought Leadership with their peers and within their social networks. With this in mind, you should prompt readers to share your white paper and make it as easy as possible for them do so. While many people like to be led by the hand, others will be grateful of the opportunity to be seen sharing your incisive content (perhaps thinking of themselves as connected Thought Leaders within their own peer group).

While you will want to collect as much useful data as possible from the individuals downloading your white paper content, be careful that you don't put people off by asking for too much personal information. The only mandatory fields in your subscription form should be the name and email address fields. You can use social media tools such as LinkedIn or Facebook to research names and email addresses and from this information potentially work out if the downloader is a hot lead or not. The name and email address will also give you enough detail to send future personalised email marketing campaigns. Details such as company name, telephone number, postal address and turnover are useful, but they are not essential at this stage and can easily be researched at a later date.

For an example of how I personally use white papers to drive leads and deliver insight check out the iContact website for a free guide (**www.icontact.com/email-marketing**).

Warning – check your website's capability

Before you distribute a white paper via your own website, you should check with your hosting company that you have sufficient bandwidth to handle a significant number of downloads. Failure to do this, especially if your white paper proves to be a particular success, may result in your hosting costs going through the roof, or worse still, your website going down completely. A broken website is the enemy of Thought Leadership. The chances of getting a visitor to return to a website that didn't work on their first visit will be slim. Don't let a powerful, and potentially lucrative, white paper destroy your website.

Promoting your white paper

You'll want to distribute your white paper as widely as possible. Your website is perhaps the most obvious starting point for promotion. Having a dedicated page for white papers is a good idea, as this will act as a central resource for your Thought Leadership. You'll also want to dedicate a significant amount of space on your home page to promote your latest white paper. However, depending on the reach of your website, the level of publicity this activity offers will be limited.

A good blog post, guest editorial or press release can help you break out of the confines of your own website and help spread your white paper across the social networks such as Facebook, Twitter and LinkedIn (we'll go into social media in greater depth in Chapter 4). Email also provides an excellent way of promoting your white papers to your existing database of customers, prospects and other interested parties.

Many companies promote their white papers by buying advertising space on third-party websites and in trade magazines. In my experience, the volume of downloads this generates can be quite small and therefore should be seen as more of a branding exercise. Unless you have budget for brand advertising, this is probably not a route you should consider.

Of course, the internet isn't the only way to distribute white papers. Printed copies make for excellent giveaways at trade shows and events, and will certainly do more to raise your profile than the usual catch-key-type giveaways like stress balls and key rings that still seem so popular. If you are going down the print route, don't skimp on design or print quality, and display your white papers as if they are premium quality magazines. A lot of thought has gone into their production, so don't give them away like you would a no-value key ring.

Extending the life and reach of your white paper

The useful, lead-generating lifespan of a white paper will vary depending on your industry and a number of other factors, such as seasonality and, never forget, the quality of your message. In a fast moving industry such as e-commerce, a great white paper might only remain relevant for a number of months. In a more mature or traditional industry the relevancy of your message might be significantly longer. But just because a white paper isn't driving a significant number of leads any more, it does not mean you should kill it off.

After I have squeezed almost every last ounce of value out of a white paper via my website, email campaigns, social media, PR, etc., I like to push it out to the internet and allow it to passively build brand awareness, reputation and generate the occasional lead as people stumble across it on their search for related topics.

There are a number of websites where you can host and share white papers. My personal favourite is Scribd (**www.scribd.com**). Scribd describes itself as the world's largest social reading and publishing company. Essentially it makes it easy for people to share and discover content across a range of formats, including PDF, Word and PowerPoint. Scribd allows you to upload and tag your content with relevant keywords, helping browsers find your white paper. The site is also extensively indexed by Google, meaning your white paper, which may have previously been hidden behind a registration page, becomes highly discoverable. Because Scribd displays content in a standard web browser, it also means your content is available across a range of devices.

With the advent of tablet computers like the iPad, and eBook readers such as Amazon's Kindle, there is a growing trend to reposition white papers as downloadable books or eBooks. The lines between the two media are blurring in terms of length, distribution channels and even price, with many Thought Leaders choosing to give book content away for free. However, I'd like to draw the line between the two media by suggesting the following: while every Thought Leader should have a number of white papers in them, very few will have a book in them.

Books/eBooks

When I consider how important a book can be to the perception of a Thought Leader, I often cast my mind back to my first meeting with ChannelAdvisor. The salesperson was running late. He'd lost his BlackBerry on the train from London and couldn't phone ahead to warn me about his late arrival. By the time he arrived I was pretty grumpy and would have been fairly resistant to his sales pitch. That is until he gave me a book written by his CEO, Scot Wingo.

As someone who had paid off a significant chunk of their mortgage by writing newspaper and magazine articles but (until now) never had the motivation to write a book, I was instantly impressed. You should never underestimate the commitment it takes to write a book, especially if you're holding down a day job and have family commitments to juggle (while writing this book I have lost count how many times I have seen the wrong side of midnight as I try and meet a self-imposed deadline).

I enjoyed Scot Wingo's book and learned a great deal from it. I was impressed that a CEO had gone to so much effort to assure me that his organisation was at the forefront of the industry. This was, in my opinion, Thought Leadership Marketing at its finest. I became a customer and when I got the chance to work for them, I jumped at it. Had it not been for Scot's book, things might have worked out very differently.

Have you got a book in you?

Before you put pen to paper, it is imperative you lay the groundwork. You might be able to pull off a blog post or a white paper without much forethought, but a book needs in-depth planning.

When planning your book you'll want to think about the following:

- **A working title:** Come up with something that will guide your writing and then leave well alone until you've finished the book, by which time something far more suitable will undoubtedly present itself.

- **A breakdown of chapters:** Include draft titles, a brief synopsis of each chapter and a list of any sub-sections or topics you will include.

- **A competitive analysis:** A list of similar titles, highlighting how your book will differ from the competition. Include details like publication date, length, sales rank on Amazon, publisher and price. This information will help you position your title competitively.

This will not only help you write the book, it will help you find a suitable publisher for your work (if you want to go down the traditional publisher route).

Finding a publisher

There are many benefits to working with a traditional publisher. First and foremost, the credibility a legitimate publisher gives your work is invaluable. Secondly, and this cannot be underestimated, the professional editorial services that a publisher provides will ensure your work is polished and showcases your Thought Leadership with maximum effect. Finally, a good publisher will get your work into the shops, solicit reviews and help with publicity (although you should also be prepared to do your own legwork in this direction).

You should start your search for a publisher before you start writing your book. This might seem a little counterintuitive but there is a very good reason for this, which is that most publishers don't like receiving unsolicited manuscripts. In the UK, *The Writers' and Artists' Yearbook* provides an excellent resource for researching suitable publishing companies. Alternatively, you can use Amazon to research publishing companies that publish books in your area of expertise.

Once you have drawn up a shortlist of suitable publishers, visit their websites and carefully read the submission guidelines. Thankfully, many business publishers will be happy to deal directly with authors, so you shouldn't worry too much about employing the services of an agent.

Submitting a book proposal is a little bit like applying for a job. You'll need to create a short covering letter which should be sent along with a brief biography, a synopsis of your proposed work (this is where your early planning will come in useful) and a sample of your work (this could be an early chapter of your book).

If a publisher shows interest in your work, it is likely they will suggest changes to the idea, which is another reason why it is not good to deliver a completed manuscript in the first instance. But remember you are the Thought Leader and it is your reputation at stake. If you are not comfortable with the suggested changes then you should push back. If you are unable to agree on the full content of your book with a particular publisher, then it is time to walk away and either find a more suitable match or consider alternative options.

Publishing deals are lengthy and complicated documents. If you are lucky enough to be presented with one, it is highly recommended you run them past a legal advisor before you sign on the dotted line. Foner Books (**www.fonerbooks.com/contract.htm**) offers some good discussion points (but not legal advice) around what is normally found in a publishing contract.

Self-publishing

Not to be confused with vanity publishing (where the author pays to have a work published), self-publishing has come a long way in recent years.

There are a number of highly-respectable self-publishing platforms that allow authors to create professional and polished products, and also make it easy to distribute your work via all the major online retailers, high street, independent booksellers and even libraries. Advances in publishing technology, such as print on demand (POD) and eBooks (digital, downloadable books that are read on electronic readers like the Kindle or iPad), mean that self-publishers (and many traditional publishers) no longer have to commit to large print runs to make projects cost-effective.

The fact that print on demand books are not actually printed until they are sold means you should never have money tied up in unsold inventory or warehousing, which again will drastically reduce the risk in producing your own books. They are also available indefinitely, meaning your Thought Leadership will never go out of print (unless you wish to retire it).

Self-publishing will enable you to publish very quickly, retain full control of your copy, allow for the publishing of niche topics that traditional publishers might not consider profitable enough to take on board and help retain a larger percentage of any royalties you might receive.

Print on demand (POD) and eBook publishing platforms

Here are a selection of POD and self-publishing platforms:

- **CreateSpace (Createspace.com):** A POD self-publishing platform owned by the online retailer Amazon. As well as the obvious advantages this company has in putting your book for sale on the world's largest online bookstore, it is also incredibly easy to set up your titles, design professional looking covers with their template driven software and extend the distribution of your book to global Amazon sites, as well as the other major online, high street and independent book retailers.

- **Kindle Direct Publishing (kdp.amazon.com):** KDP is another platform owned by Amazon, this time dedicated to publishing via the Kindle eReader. If you have any doubts about the validity of eBooks, consider this – Kindle eBooks now outsell paperback titles on Amazon. Publishing via KDP is both quick and efficient. A correctly formatted book can be available for sale across many of Amazon's international sites within 24 hours of publishing. KDP also allows self-publishers to enrol in a programme called KDP Select (**kdp.amazon.com/self-publishing/KDPSelect**) which enters your book into Amazon's free lending programme and pays a royalty from the shared pool of cash.

- **Lulu (Lulu.com):** Lulu offers a Print on Demand and eBook distribution service to Apple's iBookstore and Barnes & Noble's Nook eReader. Lulu offers a very active community forum which, in my experience, offers superior support than their official support channels.

- **Smashwords (Smashwords.com):** A solution for distributing eBooks to the Apple iBookstore, Barnes & Noble's Nook eReader, the Kobo eReader (which will also get your book listed on the WHSmith website in the UK) and the Sony eReader store. Smashwords' founder Mark Cocker is a bit of a Thought Leader in the field of eBook publishing and is definitely worth following via his blog at **blog.smashwords.com** or on Twitter **@markcoker**.

- **Google Books (books.google.com):** As part of their mission to digitise the entire world and fight Amazon and Apple for their share of the eBook market (although it has a long way to go before it makes a significant dent in these markets), Google have poured significant resources into digitising millions of out of print and classic titles. It is also possible to upload and sell your books via the Google eBookstore, which makes eBooks available via a number of devices including a wide range of eReaders, smart phones, tablets and computers via web browser-based readers. While sales from the Google eBookstore might not be currently setting the world on fire, it is highly likely that uploading your book to the Google eBookstore will benefit your title in terms of its ranking in the Google search results.

You should consider maximising the reach of your Thought Leadership by utilising more than one of the above solutions and so widening the number of distribution channels for your title. While it is highly likely that the majority of sales will come from either Amazon or the Apple iBookstore, the cumulative sales from the likes of Barnes & Noble, Kobo, Google and Sony (as well as paperback sales via traditional booksellers) will be worth the effort of setting up the additional distribution channels.

Indie Not Amateur

It is important to remember .... if you do go down the self-publishing route, that your book deserves all the care and attention it would receive from a traditional publisher. Never trust yourself to proofread your own manuscript! It is a virtually impossible task and you will miss glaring errors that make your book look cheap and amateurish. Some of the self-publishing platforms offer editorial and design services which will add a professional polish to your work. It may also be possible to find support via individuals on the various community forums and websites around the self-publishing space.

Pricing your Thought Leadership book

There are a few different ways you might want to look at how you price your book. Do you give the book away for free, sell it cheaply in the hope of attracting a significant number of sales, or ask a reasonable price and hope to earn a respectable royalty for each and every sale made?

- **Free:** With a traditional print title there is a cost associated with printing and distributing your book. This shouldn't prevent you from giving away free copies to loyal customers and hot leads. However, with the advent of the eBook which has no production costs after the original title has been set up and negligible distribution costs, the ability to circulate your book freely and widely has never been more affordable. Free eBooks are (for obvious reasons) devoured in huge numbers and can be distributed easily via the iBookstore, Barnes & Noble's Nook, Kobo and Sony eBook stores very easily by selecting Smashwords to act as your distribution mechanism. It can be a little trickier to list your title for free via the Amazon Kindle store. However, the excellent Smashwords comes to the rescue again allowing you to publish Kindle friendly (.mobi) files which can be given away either from the Smashwords site or even your own website (as you would with a white paper). To guarantee the maximum number of readers you should consider giving your work away for free. Before you decide whether or not to give your book away for free you'll have to decide what the main purpose of your Thought Leadership is. Did you write your book to demonstrate your expertise in a given field and therefore drive more business your way? Or were you hoping to supplement your business income with royalties from the sale of your book?

- **Low cost:** Again this is probably more relevant to the eBook market than the traditional dead tree variety. There is a great deal of debate about eBook pricing, with many pundits suggesting that low prices yield high results. This is perhaps more true in the arena of fiction where 99p books fly off the shelves of Amazon, Apple, etc. However, if you are delivering detailed Thought Leadership to a niche audience, pricing your book at such a low cost might put you at a disadvantage, with potential readers equating low cost with low value. Before opting for the low cost option, you'll need to evaluate the size of your audience, the competitive landscape (i.e. how much do similar Thought Leadership titles in your field sell for) and how value is perceived in your industry. A book about crafting and hobbies might appear a reasonable investment when priced at £2.99, whereas a book on high-end yacht maintenance may appear a little cheap and therefore unworthy at a similar price.

- **Reasonably priced:** You may want to earn some money from sales of your book and as such wish to charge a fair price for it. When considering this, if you are selling an eBook you should be wary about pricing yourself out of sales from an audience who might expect lower than print prices for digital content. You will also want to consider how much you hope to earn (if anything) from the publication of your eBook. To put things into perspective, Amazon currently pays self publishers a 70% commission on Kindle books priced at £2.99 or more, meaning you will earn a cool £4.89 on every £6.99 book you sell – far more than you would expect from a traditional sale of a paperback title through a publisher.

Shorter reads are blurring the lines between white papers and the book

The low costs associated with distributing eBooks via services like Amazon or the Apple iBookstore have helped authors redefine exactly what a book is. While a traditional Thought Leadership book might be anywhere between 20,000 to 40,000 words in length, new eBook distribution channels allow for much shorter works to be distributed cost effectively and even profitably. This means the lines between what you might consider a detailed white paper and the book are beginning to blur, and the available distribution channels for your Thought Leadership are expanding.

Spread the word – the gospel according to you

No matter how you publish, you should be prepared to promote your book wherever you go. As a Thought Leader, being remembered as the person who wrote the book about your particular line of business is great for your reputation. Remember, while many people talk about having a book in them, not many people will have the stuff to actually sit down and write one. If you are one of these people, it's time to separate yourself from the crowd, get to work and be prepared to shout about it after you have finished.

Finally, if you think you have a book in you but just haven't got the time to sit down and write one, consider this; you only need to find the time to write 250 words per day and within four months you'll have 30,000 words on paper. Alternatively you could consider the option of hiring a ghost writer. Refer back to Chapter 2 for the pros and cons of this option and remember a full-length ghost written book will involve a considerable investment of money and time to guarantee a product that you will be proud of.

Video

If time really is an issue and you want to get your point of view out in a quick and efficient manner to as wide an audience as possible, you should consider using video. Video is the most effective tool for humanising your Thought Leadership. People tend to buy off people they like and if they have never met you before, video is a great medium for allowing potential customers to look you in the eye, take your advice and decide whether or not they could do business with you.

I have worked with large-scale video production companies and also produced extremely low-cost video campaigns with nothing more sophisticated than a Flip video camera on top of a cheap tripod. Your approach will depend on your budget, the production values you desire, the strength of your message and the speed you hope to reach the market with your video.

Here are some ideas of what you might use video for.

Six great ideas to commit to video

1. **Customer success stories:** Case studies are perhaps the easiest and most effective videos to make. Potential clients will be keen to see and hear how existing customers have benefited from using your services. If you don't want to appear on camera yourself, customer success stories present an opportunity to stay behind the lens. Questions can be posed by title cards (just like in old fashioned silent movies) which can also be used to break up the footage and act as dividers between edits. Remember, you'll never get three minutes of clean footage (and with a case study you won't want much more than that), so plan to ask a lot of questions and be prepared to edit down.

2. **Product/service demonstrations:** Sometimes it is far easier to show a potential customer what they can do with your product or service than try to explain in words.

3. **Product/service reviews:** Casting a critical eye over the products and services that your customers might find useful will demonstrate your understanding of their industry and solidify your reputation.

4. **Public speaking/lectures:** A great example of how you can extend the reach of and recycle your Thought Leadership. This is one situation where you cannot expect to turn up at an event and point a camcorder at the stage and come away with useable video – it will (and I defy you to prove me wrong) look awful. Events are best filmed using well-lit stages, multiple cameras and some heavy duty editing.

5. **Whiteboard presentations:** A video blending the general concept of the product demonstration and public speaking video. This essentially places the Thought Leader and a whiteboard in front of a camera to freestyle a presentation and explain a particular concept.

6. **Vlogging:** Taking the concept of blogging into the video age. This is essentially where you replace written blog posts with video posts. This will be particularly useful for people working in highly visual industries such as, but certainly not limited to, fashion, sport, entertainment, travel or real estate.

Hosting your videos on YouTube

The video hosting site YouTube (**www.youtube.com**) is the most obvious venue for hosting your Thought Leadership videos for a number of reasons:

- **It's free:** You couldn't find a better price point.

- **It's owned by Google:** This will do no harm in helping people find your videos.

- **It's one of the most popular sites on the internet:** See above.

- **It allows you to create your own branded channel:** You'll have a central repository for all your Thought Leadership videos.

- **It makes distribution easy:** YouTube videos can be embedded easily into your own website or shared across the social network sites like Facebook.

- **It can offer an additional stream of revenue:** YouTube selects popular video producers and shares advertising revenue with them.

You should host your videos on YouTube for all the above reasons. But you might also want to consider other options as your primary host (i.e. the service you use to host videos on your own website) because YouTube also has a number of disadvantages:

- **Branding cannot be removed:** The YouTube branding is always displayed even when the video is embedded on your website. Depending on your own branding, this may appear intrusive or just plain vulgar.

- **Random opening screen:** You are unable to select the precise (perfect) image which is displayed as your opening screen on your embedded video player. This might result in a completely unsuitable image such as a still of a person with their eyes shut or mouth wide open.

- **Potential for conflicting advertisements:** You have no control over the advertising displayed next to your videos and this might result in your competitors' adverts running alongside your Thought Leadership.

YouTube alternatives

There are numerous alternative video sharing websites available. Wikipedia provides a useful and near complete comparison of service providers
(**en.wikipedia.org/wiki/Comparison_of_video_services**).
However, in my own personal experience I have found the two most business-friendly video sites to be Vimeo (**www.vimeo.com**) and Vzaar (**www.vzaar.com**). Both of these sites offer paid subscription services, which gives you the additional control over your videos that is not currently offered by YouTube.

Video Podcasting via iTunes

Apple's iTunes also provides an excellent distribution tool for your video content, particularly when presented as part of a series of video podcasts (or Vodcasts as they are often referred to). Although the headline grabbing days of podcasting are perhaps long gone, they are still a popular and highly accessible method of communicating with a global audience.

By submitting your video podcast to iTunes you allow owners of video enabled iPods, iPhones and iPads (and there are many millions of them) to easily subscribe to your Thought Leadership content. One of the added advantages of building a subscription base via a service like iTunes is that subsequent Thought Leadership podcasts are automatically delivered to your subscribers, giving you multiple opportunities to influence and impress. For this reason, you should try to update your podcasts on a fairly regular basis (**www.apple.com/itunes**).

Having said that, as with any other form of Thought Leadership Marketing, the quality of the content is far more important than your publishing, or in this case podcasting, schedule. If you don't have anything relevant or interesting to say, wait until you do.

Podcasting is a little more complicated than uploading a video to YouTube. You will need to:

- Ensure your video is saved as a supported file format.

- Host your video somewhere on the internet (be aware you may need to ensure your hosting package has ample bandwidth to cope with the demands of hosting and delivering large files).

- Create an RSS Feed and a unique URL (website address).

If this all sounds a little daunting there is an easy-to-follow podcasting guide available from Apple (**www.apple.com/itunes/podcasts**).

Don't forget audio

Audio podcasts are also popular and much easier to produce than their video counterparts (as well as sparing the blushes of the camera shy). Audio podcasts can be consumed during otherwise dead time, such as driving or while walking the dog – when watching a video would not be possible – and therefore offers busy people the opportunity to catch up with their Thought Leadership education anytime, anywhere. Remember, many people like to make important decisions away from the working environment and a simple audio podcast can be the ideal medium to reach these people when they are doing something else.

Public speaking/events

Speaking at industry events is the perfect way to cement your reputation as a talented and knowledgeable Thought Leader. It is also perhaps the most daunting aspect of Thought Leadership Marketing. Very few people are born natural public speakers, and even the most experienced speaker will get a little nervous before standing in front of a room full of strangers or, perhaps more intimidating, a room of industry peers.

As with all public performances, as well as many other aspects of Thought Leadership Marketing, practice makes perfect; so you should be prepared to dive right in and try to keep any stage fright in check. It might take some time to find your natural flow and build a unique style into your presentations, but when you find it you'll know you've got it and public speaking will become, if not an absolute pleasure, certainly more enjoyable.

Getting the gig

Throughout the year there will be countless opportunities to present your Thought Leadership at a wide range of industry events and trade shows. But here is the rub – getting the gig, particularly if you don't have a big company name behind you, can be very difficult.

Most regular events will provide details on submitting your application (often referred to as a 'call for papers') to speak. Normally you will have to complete a simple form with a brief synopsis of your presentation, a personal biography, details of any case studies you will be referring to in the session and any co-presenters. Co-presenters, particularly when they are associated with big name brands, are influential in securing speaking opportunities. Event organisers will more often than not give preferential treatment to paid exhibitors. If you have the budget and the desire to exhibit at an event, factoring in a guaranteed speaking slot can be a useful bargaining chip when negotiating the cost of your exhibition stand or booth.

If your speaking application is accepted, the organisers will probably require some additional information, such as high resolution photographs of the speakers and good quality logos to help them promote your session via the event website, as well as any printed guides and advertisements. They will normally also ask for any presentation materials (i.e. a pithy PowerPoint presentation, along with any special materials such as video) to be supplied in good time for the event.

There is a good reason for this – the event organisers will not only want to line your presentation up correctly with the schedule, they will also want to check the formatting of your deck and ensure that it is compatible with the hardware/software used on the day. It's in your best interest to be prepared. When you hand your presentation in at the last minute you run the risk of things going wrong when you are at your most vulnerable; on stage and in front of an audience.

The 80/20 rule

I'm a great believer in the 80/20 rule for public speaking. My own version of the Pareto principle calls for 80% planning and 20% chaos. You should always plan for a little chaos in your presentations. If a speech is completely planned and rehearsed it may appeared staid and uninspiring. Remember people buy from people they like, so try and be likeable. By factoring in a little chaos you should be prepared to take your presentation a little off-piste (although be careful not to stray too far from the topic) when the opportunity arises. Your audience will dictate when this happens. It'll also help you with any off-topic or particularly difficult questions.

On the subject of difficult questions, if you really cannot (or do not want to) answer them in a public forum, try and push back in a manner that will not reflect badly on you. Suggest, for the sake of offering a worthy answer and allowing time for further questions, that you find some time to chat in greater depth after your presentation and quickly move on. If you simply do not know the answer, tell the audience you don't have the precise details to hand and make the suggestion to follow up at a later date.

Death by PowerPoint

Many public speakers rely too much on PowerPoint slides to support them during their presentations. While a good deck of slides will undoubtedly act as a visual stimulant for your audience and a prompt for you, a bad deck will confuse, distract and potentially bore your audience. Remember, people have come to hear you speak, not squint and hurriedly copy notes (or tweet) from your slides as you flick backwards and forwards through them.

I regularly see people at events taking photographs and even specifically videoing slide decks as they are rattled through by the presenter. Can you imagine how potentially damaging these shakily shot pictures and videos can become to your reputation if uploaded to the internet without any real quality control or context?

You can go some way to prevent this from happening by (a) keeping your slides nice and simple and (b) promising your audience a free copy of a much more detailed piece of Thought Leadership at the end of your presentation. This is a great method of maximising the engagement with your audience, collecting contact details and distributing a prepared item, such as a white paper or eBook.

Practice makes perfect (without growing up in public)

To build your confidence in your public speaking ability you'll need to get up on a stage and start presenting. But jumping in at the deep end is not always the best idea. You don't want to make your early career mistakes in front of a crowd of red hot prospects or industry peers. Thankfully, it is possible to hone your craft in front of a more forgiving audience without risking your reputation.

Organisations like the Rotary Club, the Women's Institute and local business networking clubs often invite speakers to present at their regular meetings. By engaging with such organisations, you will have the opportunity to cut your teeth in front of an educated, potentially business-minded, but above all friendly, audience. This approach will make you concentrate on how to communicate effectively to an audience who might not be knowledgeable about your particular line of business. This will stand you in good stead when you move up a league or two.

Even when you are speaking to a more informed audience, you should always aim to speak plainly and clearly. Remember, unexplained industry-specific jargon is the weapon of choice for the ill-informed who do not really know a subject. You might think it makes you look big and clever, but in reality all it does is exclude and confuse and these are not words you should associate with Thought Leadership.

Even the big guys can fail

Lack of preparation can make you look very foolish indeed. I have been lucky enough to see senior managers from many of the world's largest internet and technology companies (including the likes of Facebook, eBay, Amazon, Google, Saleforce and Magento) present at conferences all over Europe and the United States. Normally these presentations have been, as you would expect, highly professional and polished. However, on one occasion I saw an executive (who I won't name) from one of these top companies drop the ball completely and pretty much make a fool of himself in front of 300 people.

The session was at best ambitious, blending a standard PowerPoint presentation, video and a live online demonstration. The problem came when the presenter needed to login to a simple online application (just as you would every day with your email) and he forgot the password. The trial account had been set up by someone else and he had no way of retrieving the login information. That was it, the presentation was over. He tried his best to explain what the "easy-to-use" online application would do, if only he was able to get into it, but he fell flat on his face and finished his presentation with an apology. Not a great position to find yourself in if you want to be perceived as a Thought Leader.

I'm sure we've all seen things go wrong with presentations. The secret is to rely on yourself and not technology to get the message across.

In my mind, the best presentations are when one or more people stand on a stage together and communicate with the audience with as little reliance on slide decks or other multimedia presentations as possible.

If you are struggling to come up with a presentation style that is both colourful and detailed, without relying too much on the big screens behind you, try downloading an audio podcast from a Thought Leader you admire or tune into the BBC World Service and discover the power of free flowing speech with no distracting images.

Organising your own events

Organising your own events can be a great way to meet your existing and potential clients, provide a platform for your Thought Leadership and generate a little PR buzz around your business. Self-run events don't have to break the bank and, depending on your objectives, might even provide a stream of revenue for your business.

Depending on the scale of your event you may want to hire the services of an event management company who can help you with finding a venue, ticketing and AV (audio and visuals), all the way through to complete event management and staffing. But this doesn't mean you cannot take on running small events by yourself or perhaps with the help of a friendly client or business partner.

Finding a venue can be the trickiest and most costly aspect of organising your own event. Most hotels (of a reasonable size) will offer meeting and conference rooms for hire. These, particularly in large cities, can be very expensive. Most venues are hired out either for a flat fee, with an additional charge made for refreshments and any extras, or as a day delegate package, which covers the room and any pre-arranged extras. In the current economy, the events industry has, like many other businesses, been hit hard in the pocket. Use this to your advantage and be prepared to haggle over costs. You might be surprised what you can get away with.

Thinking outside of the box with regards to finding a suitable venue can help you reduce costs. Universities, colleges, schools and even local libraries often have meeting rooms which can be hired by the hour at much lower rates than the more traditional corporate venues.

Selling tickets

Services like the excellent Eventbrite (**www.eventbrite.com**) offers an incredibly simple and cost-effective online ticketing solution. The service is free for any free events and there is a 2.5% + $0.99 fee per ticket if you wish to charge for your event. As well as providing a robust platform for setting up and promoting your event via email,

Eventbrite integrates easily with credit card services like PayPal and works with multiple currencies.

Sharing costs

It is always a good idea to work with a trusted partner or two when organising an event. Not only can they help share the costs, they can also help promote and sell the tickets and, perhaps even more importantly, give you a much needed break while they present, giving you the opportunity to mingle with your delegates.

Calculating the value of events

It can be difficult to estimate the value or importance of events to your business, and as a result too many companies fail to successfully track data beyond the number of new customers acquired through events. Some don't even do this and so spend their events budget blindly.

As well as the value of sales generated from events, you should consider the following points:

- What is the value of any PR generated from the publicity around your event?

- How important to your brand is it to be seen in a recognised arena alongside your competitors and suppliers?

- How many existing clients do you retain through your contact with them at events?

- How many great ideas do your clients and prospects share with you? Perhaps more importantly, how do you record these ideas and act on them at a later date?

Surveying delegates

It is always a good idea to survey your delegates at the end of an event. This can give you feedback on everything from the standard of the presentations and Thought Leadership materials, all the way through to the quality of the venue and catering (to some of your delegates this will be more important than the actual content).

On the subject of catering, if you are offering anything more complex than an endless supply of coffee and biscuits always enquire about special dietary requirements and act accordingly. Failure to provide a Kosher, Halal or vegan meal might (as I have learned through personal experience) cause offence, or at the very least be embarrassing to your delegate (whether they tell you or not).

A small group of delegates can be surveyed prior to leaving your event. Encourage them to complete a quick survey with the promise of a post-event drink, which will also provide a last chance for a networking opportunity. For larger groups you might want to consider an online survey tool such as SurveyMonkey (**www.surveymonkey.com**). To guarantee a higher number of returned surveys you should think about offering an incentive, such as a prize draw or discount voucher.

It might seem a little obvious to say, but if you go to the bother of surveying your delegates, don't forget to follow up on the results. You will rarely be given the opportunity to learn so much about what your clients and prospects think about doing business with you. Take note, learn and make appropriate changes. Survey results can also provide some excellent content to feature on your website, blog or any other channel where you promote your Thought Leadership.

Webinars

Webinars offer a cost effective and rapidly deployed alternative to organising a physical event. A webinar is a virtual event hosted online and accessed either by telephone or by a web-enabled device (occasionally both). Webinar software such as GoToMeeting (**www.gotomeeting.com**) allows you to quickly and easily host audio/visual presentations, sharing items like PowerPoint presentations or software demonstrations running on your computer with your webinar attendees. Webinar software also allows your attendees to participate with Q&A via online text-based chat facilities, or voice via phone or their computer's microphone.

A webinar can be a regularly scheduled event showcasing a particular product or idea with a handful of attendees or a major one-off marketing event with multiple presenters and many hundreds of virtual delegates.

Five reasons why you should consider running webinars

1. **Extremely cost effective:** Events can be very expensive once you have factored in all the costs. Room hire, AV, staging, travel, catering, etc.; it all adds up. Webinar technology provides the opportunity to stage large-scale presentations at a fraction of the cost of physical events.

2. **Environmentally friendly:** As well as the financial burden of running a physical event, you shouldn't underestimate the environmental cost of getting all your delegates and presenters to the same conference facility.

3. **Brings people together across large distances:** Your presenters and delegates don't have to be in the same room. They don't even have to be on the same continent.

4. **Recycling your Thought Leadership:** Webinars can be recorded and recycled as podcasts or YouTube videos.

5. **Highly trackable marketing:** Most webinar software comes with a built-in suite of marketing tools allowing you to promote and follow up on your event with email.

Joined-up thinking

Thought Leadership channels work best when they are operated as part of a complete multi-channel strategy and so you should try and combine as many of these channels as you can. Remember, one channel often feeds the other, so try and plan your content to suit as many channels as you can. Don't overstretch yourself, but do try and put yourself out there with a fairly robust campaign.

While the aforementioned channels will supply you with fairly good coverage, it is by no means a comprehensive list. My advice is to get these tried and tested channels working for you first before looking to expand into new areas. If you find a particular channel works well for you, whether featured in this book or not, I'd love to hear about your success.

Calculating the value of PR

Calculating the true value of your PR efforts can be a little tricky.

One of the most common methods that public relations firms use to calculate the value of PR is by using a formula known as advertising value equivalent (AVE). AVE measures the physical space an article takes up in a print publication, or the duration of broadcast time for TV or radio, and compares this to the medium's advertising rate card. This value is then often multiplied by two or three, and occasionally even up to seven times, to represent the true value of the PR. This works on the assumption that won media is far more valuable than paid advertising.

There are of course a number of flaws in calculating the value of PR using AVE. Advertising rate cards are an inexact method for calculating the value of space, because few advertisers will actually ever pay at rate card levels, making it very hard to judge the real value of space. The value of a win can also be significantly altered by the general sentiment of the article and the quality of the contribution. Also, what if the media doesn't have a rate card, like the BBC?

And then there is the question of online media. Website operators tend to value their advertising by looking at a metric, normally measured over a cost per thousand (CPM) page impressions. This metric can vary wildly and once an article goes live online – unless you have the technology in place (check out **www.vocus.com**) to monitor impressions – you will have difficulty understanding how many times it has been seen.

The only way of truly understanding the value of your PR is by measuring the leads that are generated from your efforts and tracking any conversions. While this might be possible using online media tools like Google Analytics (**www.google.com/analytics**) or a customer relationship management (CRM) tool like **Salesforce.com**, when you factor in traditional media, such as print, TV or radio, you may find it harder to keep track of things.

Social media is also a valuable tool for studying the reach of your PR efforts. We'll be looking into social media in much more depth in Chapter 4, where we will examine the concept of social media monitoring.

If you are managing your own PR, I recommend you use a mix of analytics, social media and raw gut feeling (based on an increase in telephone and email enquiries) to gauge the success of your activity. If you are working with an agency, it's probably best to take any estimate of the value of your PR with a pinch of salt.

I'll leave you with a final thought on how you really should perceive the true value of your public relations activity. If the phone isn't ringing and the sales aren't coming in, your PR isn't as valuable as you might think (or some people would have you believe) it is.

Chapter 4

Using Social Media to Position Yourself as a Thought Leader

've already mentioned the following point but I believe it is very important, so please forgive the repetition – maintaining a social media presence does not make you a Thought Leader. In fact, it is more likely to identify you as a wannabe if you do not get your content-led (not socially-led) strategy via the various channels discussed in the previous chapter right first.

Social media is a vast and ever expanding universe. Entire volumes have been dedicated to single social media platforms. While this book can only touch on the surface of the medium, it does focus on perhaps one of the most important and rarely highlighted facts. Social media is not at all complicated (your kids are probably all over it). Like many other aspects of Thought Leadership Marketing, common sense is the most active ingredient.

For the sake of this book I will focus on the four most prominent social media channels in the UK and the US. These are:

1. Facebook (**www.facebook.com**)

2. Twitter (**www.twitter.com**)

3. Google+ (**plus.google.com**)

4. My own personal favourite – LinkedIn (**www.linkedin.com**)

A quick guide to ...

... Facebook

'The Social Network' hardly needs any introduction. With more than 800 million active users you don't need to ask if your customers or competitors use it. As well as providing a very useful tool for sharing everything from simple text-based posts, to photographs, blog posts and videos with your friends, it also provides a direct channel for communication with your friends who can post directly to your wall (which is why you need to listen and respond).

More sophisticated users might want to invest in bespoke Facebook applications (pieces of software which run on the Facebook platform), allowing you to create a more flexible and interactive environment.

... Twitter

Twitter is far more impressive than its 140 character limit might suggest. Its beauty doesn't lie in its massive celebrity following, but in the fact that messages posted to its system (tweets) are instantly searchable, and are therefore instantly discoverable. As well as feeding through to your followers' Twitter feeds, the service also acts as a high-pressure hose squirting your content out, as and when it is produced, to the major search engines, including Yahoo and Bing (but not to Google at the time of writing). If you don't understand Twitter, it's time to get your head around it. It has the potential to drive more traffic to your Thought Leadership than any other medium.

... Google+

Google+ is the new kid on the social media block and the jury is still out on the opportunities it offers for Thought Leaders and businesses in general. There is, however, one solid piece of advice I can offer you regarding Google's Facebook killer: Engaging with the social network owned by the most popular and powerful search engine can do absolutely no harm to your search engine optimisation (SEO) strategy.

... LinkedIn

LinkedIn is the ultimate business social network. I have personally used it to find employment, seek out business partners, promote events, gather advice from my peers and successfully distribute a vast range of Thought Leadership content. How did people do business before LinkedIn? I honestly cannot remember and could not imagine my professional life without it.

Serious Thought Leaders should consider setting up a LinkedIn Group covering their particular area of expertise. This is a great way of positioning yourself favourably within a group of your peers and potential clients.

Social media should not be a waste of time

Social media can be a waste of time if you are not disciplined in your approach. It can literally eat hours out of your working day, leaving you working late or just plain unproductive. It's a little bit like digital quicksand; it can suck you right in. One minute you can be scanning a network for valuable nuggets of business-related information and the next you're discussing Manchester United's chances in Europe or reliving a co-worker's drunken Saturday night antics.

Social media can be habit forming, wasteful and downright dangerous. But that is also why it is so useful. It's time to harness social media and show it, and your followers, just who the boss (Thought Leader) is by following some very simple rules.

Seven golden rules for winning at social media

- **Rule 1 – Separate your work life from your family and social life:** Only use social media for work purposes during office hours. You wouldn't (or at least you shouldn't) spend hours talking about things that are not work related when you are at the office. Leave any 'social' social media activity for home or during your lunch breaks. It may be possible to socialise both work and social content on Facebook and Twitter, but I believe in keeping any fun and games off professional networks like LinkedIn. If you do use a personal Facebook or Twitter profile for business purposes as well as personal details, be careful what you share and never post when under the influence of drink.

- **Rule 2 – Maintain a standard profile across any professional social networks:** Use the same photograph or image across all your social networking profiles. This will help people quickly and easily identify you on a busy wall of information.

- **Rule 3 – Be selective in what you share:** Don't be one of the many thousands of people whose only social media activity is to re-post the same story, often published by a major news network or well-read blog, which is perhaps loosely connected to your business. It's highly unlikely that you are breaking any news here or will be inciting people to click on your links. You want to make sure that anything you share is both highly relevant and of interest to your followers. If at all possible, the shared content should be taken from your own Thought Leadership programme or a nugget of information from an individual you admire or respect (and preferably not a competitor).

- **Rule 4 – Learn to Listen:** Schedule time to listen to feedback relating to your company or brand via the social networks. Larger companies may want to employ sophisticated software such as Vocus, Radian6 or Brandwatch, but smaller companies can keep costs down by using the search facility on Twitter, monitoring their Facebook pages and setting up Google Alerts to catch mentions on blogs and forums, etc. It's also a good idea to monitor your competitors' brand terms and compare sentiment towards them with your brand.

- **Rule 5 – Be social:** It's called social media for a good reason. Instead of just broadcasting, try and interact with your audience. This is vital if you hope to build community around your Thought Leadership (see Chapter 5). Thank people for kind words or recommendations, try to assist people who might have problems and never ignore an angry comment. In the fast-paced world of social media a tiny spark of discontent can quickly turn into a wildfire – keep a check on this.

- **Rule 6 – Automate: social media operates across international borders and multiple time zones:** No matter how much of a hardcore marketer you might think you are or how much strong coffee you drink, there is no way you'll be able to maximise your social media presence without a little help. There are a number of software tools available (including iContact – **www.iContact.com**) designed to help you schedule and track your social media output. This means you can post messages to the likes of Facebook or Twitter at times when your customers are online, freeing you to dedicate your time to more important things (see Rule 1) or perhaps even sleeping, if your customers are on the other side of the world.

- **Rule 7 – Maintain momentum:** Once you have started, don't stop. An ill-tended or redundant social network gives the impression of a slack organisation, or may even suggest you have gone out of business. It might take a number of months to see any real return on your investment (in terms of followers and revenue) so stick at it and be prepared to build slowly.

Socialise your content

Social media sharing tools, such as the Facebook 'Like' button or Twitter's 'Tweet' button (which you can add to your blog or articles on your website), make it easy for people to share the Thought Leadership content on your website with their friends and followers via their own social networks. In this socially enabled age, you would be foolish to ignore the opportunity presented by these little, traffic-generating buttons. I'm constantly surprised how many website owners don't make it easy for people to share their content.

So who clicks on these little buttons and shares your content so freely across the social landscape?

Well, first of all there are the wannabes who I have previously mentioned in this book. While they think they are working to raise their profile by cleverly appropriating your content, it's actually you (and perhaps your competitors as well) they are working for. Then there are your legitimate business partners who want to give you a shout out and align their business more closely with you. There is also an army of bloggers and journalists who have perhaps stumbled across your content while researching a topic and believe your Thought Leadership adds to their credibility if they re-post it.

Finally, there is the most important group of people: your customers and your potential customers. If they are sharing your content in a positive manner then congratulations, you are doing something right and you are well on your way to becoming a Thought Leader.

Share and share alike (even your emails)

Don't restrict your social sharing to just your blog or website content. You can include social sharing buttons on virtually anything that can be hosted online, including white papers and emails.

Email marketing provides the perfect partner to your social media strategy. You should include social sharing buttons in all your email marketing messages and newsletters. iContact have a system that is very easy to use, which allows you to drop multiple social media sharing buttons into the body of your email messages. By socialising your emails in this manner you are effectively turning a marketing tool, normally associated with repeat business or retention, into an acquisition tool.

Your emails go out to your existing customer base and people who have expressed an interest in receiving information from you. You should think of these people as your brand ambassadors. These are people who endorse your product and potentially hang on your every word. If you tell these ambassadors about something interesting it is highly likely that they will want to share it. And because your ambassadors' friends and followers are likely to share similar interests, it is also likely that they will share their new found knowledge.

Don't confuse ambassadors with wannabes. An ambassador selflessly promotes your cause and offers testimony to the quality of your Thought Leadership message. A wannabe is simply out to make a name for themselves on the back of your hard-won reputation. While both the ambassador and wannabe are useful in distributing your content, they have different ideals and do not contribute the same value to the community you hope to build around your Thought Leadership.

Chapter 5

Building a Community Around Your Thought Leadership

G reat Thought Leaders cannot succeed in isolation. They need to build community around their Thought Leadership, employing an army of colleagues, brand ambassadors, business partners and even wannabes to endorse and distribute their message. A well-oiled community will help you distribute your content, share ideas and even handle customer service issues on your behalf, adding value to your Thought Leadership.

Ten tips to help you build a community around your thought leadership

1. **Always strive to produce great content:** Great Thought Leaders are never complacent when it comes to producing great content. Shoddy, ill-thought out content will not win any ringing endorsements and your community will vote with their feet.

2. **Make your ambassadors feel part of something special:** Try to involve people in your content creation. They could act as case studies, provide quotes for white papers, or you might just ask their opinion prior to the release of an item of Thought Leadership to help them feel part of the process. You could also give your ambassadors first glimpse of any new material, giving them the perception of a competitive advantage by being among the first group of people to benefit from your Thought Leadership.

3. **Engage socially:** Take the time to single out followers and friends on the various social media networks, thank them for their help, re-post their content and make them feel like a valued member of the team. The Follow Friday hashtag (**#ff**) on Twitter is a great way to show you value your followers.

4. **Learn to listen:** You cannot possibly pretend to know it all. Take the time to listen to your followers. Give them the opportunity to add value to your Thought Leadership programme by adding their comments to your blogged articles or the opportunity to speak at your events. Be prepared to take notes and try not to be offended by any criticism. This might give the opportunity for the occasional off-piste comment to infiltrate your Thought Leadership, but it may also give you your next great idea.

5. **Reward people for sharing:** For many people the mere fact they are associated with a great Thought Leader in their particular field of interest will be enough reward. However, a small cash reward for referring new clients can act as a powerful incentive to be more community spirited. This could be in the form of an affiliate or referral programme, where you pay a percentage or flat fee for a sale or a valid introduction. Or it could be something far simpler, like sending a Christmas card, birthday greeting or even just a random gift (all part of making people feel special) to your most active or helpful community members.

6. **Networking is not just about business:** Try and find time to meet with your clients, prospects and followers at industry events, or organise purely social meetings with them outside of the work environment. Have a round of golf, take them to the theatre, buy them tickets to a sport event or just have a drink with them and get to know them. Have they got kids? Where did they last go on holiday? When business and friendship collide, great communities are formed.

7. **Be a matchmaker:** If you have two clients or prospects that could benefit from working together, go out of your way to make the introduction. Be careful here and don't recommend anyone who you wouldn't want to work with yourself.

8. **Collect new friends:** Always be on the lookout for new community members. Make it as easy as possible to keep track of them once they have discovered your Thought Leadership by giving them every opportunity to either follow you via the main social networks or through an email subscription.

9. **Be likable:** Remember, people like to do business with people they like. Speak in plain English and try not to talk down to people. We all have to start somewhere and even the most inexperienced and naïve follower can develop into a valuable community member. If nothing else, their enthusiasm will be infectious.

10. **Dedicate significant time and resources to building your community:** If you cannot be bothered to commit to building community around your Thought Leadership, then why should anyone else?

Putting the power of community to work

In the online environment, many Thought Leaders put their community to work as unpaid sales advisors or customer support agents. It's hard to believe, but sometimes these virtual teams of volunteers can be more effective than your own salaried people. Online communities or forums allow users to post and answer a wide range of topics, as well as debate the most pressing industry-related issues of the day.

Huge online brands, such as eBay and Amazon, operate highly effective online communities. Regular users of these communities (a mixture of employees and customers) often become so knowledgeable about a product or service that they can identify a problem and advise a solution before you even know there is an issue. Some companies actually endorse community members as official moderators. The motivation for these moderators is perhaps the desire to build their own reputation as Thought Leaders.

Indeed, I know several people who have gone on to form reasonably successful careers as consultants, built on their reputation gained from participation within communities. Allowing your community to help each other with simple problems will free up your resources to deal with larger issues. With this in mind, you should constantly monitor your online communities and be ready to jump on anything that needs your input.

Third-party communities

Occasionally, unofficial communities targeting people interested in your business or industry, which are outside of your control, can spring up. While some of these communities will prove useful, others might just prove to be a distraction, or even downright dangerous. You'll have to make your own judgement call on whether or not you engage with these communities based on their content, search engine visibility and fellow community members. Try and take any negative comments offline and never indulge in an argument, as this will just make the conversation more visible and potentially damage your reputation even more. Any obvious rants and plain abusive posts are often best left ignored as acknowledging them will add fuel to their fire.

Empowering colleagues

There is a great deal of debate about how much freedom you should give your colleagues or employees to distribute their own brand of Thought Leadership. I personally believe giving your colleagues a voice is invaluable. It suggests that you have a smart bunch of people working with you and guarantees, to your customers, that your business is in good hands if you are not around.

This doesn't mean you should open the floodgates and let everyone within your organisation create and distribute Thought Leadership on your behalf. Any content should be on-brand and approved, in as much as you believe the person that has created it has a valid opinion, which matches the ethos of your own Thought Leadership.

New voices

Everyone within your organisation will have a different style and should present their Thought Leadership using their own voice. This is good because it will go a long way to prove that your content isn't hot housed or ghostwritten by a single entity; thus humanising your business.

Having multiple personalities within your business is also good for a number of reasons. Even as a leading authority in your industry, you cannot be expected to know every fine detail regarding every stream of your business. You can present a detailed overview and then by adding another voice, presented as coming from a specialist in a particular area, you increase the perception of knowledge.

You should, however, maintain a high level of quality control and set house rules for the public release of content. If your time does not allow for you to moderate your colleagues' content, you should appoint someone to make the decisions for you.

Empowering partners

Partners can add value to your Thought Leadership Marketing campaigns, particularly if you associate yourself with a larger or more respected brand. Large brands can also benefit from their association with smaller and perhaps more agile companies by harnessing their entrepreneurial spirit and freedom to move outside of the corporate constraints of big business.

Co-branding Thought Leadership

Combining the Thought Leadership prowess of two (or more) complementary companies creates an opportunity to generate exceptional content, with the potential of reaching a far wider audience. Try to play to the strengths of the organisations involved and make sure tasks and deadlines for producing content, any approval processes, etc., are all agreed and documented.

A clandestine meeting which produces many leads

Here is an example of how I have personally used relationships, co-branding and a little knowledge exchange to mutually benefit partner organisations.

I will not mention the names of any of the companies involved in the following story, for fear of embarrassing any former partners.

I was on my way back to my office one lunchtime when my phone buzzed with an incoming text message. I rarely get text messages (my least favourite method of communication) and so I was instantly intrigued. The message came from someone I had never met before in the marketing department of a very large international business. I was to meet them in a park close to their office and I should hurry as my coffee was getting cold (black, no sugar – how did they know?). I'd been trying to find a way in to working more closely with this company for a number of months, so I quickly changed direction and headed towards the park.

After a little small talk, my contact came straight to the point by asking what was involved in running a webinar. To be honest, I was surprised that such a senior marketer in such a large organisation didn't have the knowledge or resources to run such a simple task. So, I took the bull by the horns and calmly told them I wasn't going to tell them.

Instead, I told them that I would organise the webinar for them. They would provide and deliver the content and pick up any costs associated with the event, which I would book and raise an invoice for. I would do the legwork marketing the session and guide them through the technical process. The webinar and all content was to be co-branded and I would introduce and close the session. This would firmly cement the association between our two companies and give me great Thought Leadership content with very little real effort.

While I believed organising a webinar was a lot easier than producing detailed content, my partner company felt completely the opposite.

We shared all the leads. This, I believe, is a great example of a win-win situation and demonstrates how a little shared knowledge goes a long way.

Conclusion

Your First Steps Towards Thought Leadership

So you've read the book, I hope you are more than a little inspired to take the next steps towards Thought Leadership.

By now you should understand:

- What Thought Leadership Marketing is
- Who can benefit from Thought Leadership Marketing (YOU!!!)
- The various channels used to distribute Thought Leadership
- The best practices around these channels
- How to understand the true value of your Thought Leadership Marketing campaigns
- How to maximise your potential via social media
- How to empower your clients, colleagues, business partners and build a community.

Final thought

I'd like to leave you with the following thought:

I cannot tell you how to run your business. I can only offer you a little advice on how to maximise your reputation within your particular industry. You already know your customers, your products and your services. I'm sure you already deliver detailed insight into your craft or business function in your everyday working life. The chances are you are already a highly skilled Thought Leader.

Now you know this, what are you waiting for?

Go out and tell the world and when you have succeeded in creating a truly valuable Thought Leadership programme come back and let me know – I'd love to feature a case study from you in a future book.

Now when someone asks you for a penny for your thoughts, you can reply, "No chance. They could be worth millions".

John W. Hayes
@john_w_hayes

eBook edition

As a buyer of the print edition of *Becoming THE Expert* you
can now download the eBook edition free of charge to read
on an eBook reader, your smartphone or your computer.
Simply go to:

http://ebooks.harriman-house.com/thoughtleadership

or point your smartphone at the QRC below.

You can then register and download your eBook copy of the book.

www.harriman-house.com